URIAH

Uriah Phillips Levy, Captain, USN, and the Naval Court of Inquiry

Edited by
Mel Young

University Press of America,® Inc.
Lanham · Boulder · New York · Toronto · Plymouth, UK

Copyright © 2009 by
University Press of America,® Inc.
4501 Forbes Boulevard
Suite 200
Lanham, Maryland 20706
UPA Acquisitions Department (301) 459-3366

Estover Road
Plymouth PL6 7PY
United Kingdom

All rights reserved
Printed in the United States of America
British Library Cataloging in Publication Information Available

Library of Congress Control Number: 2008938256
ISBN-13: 978-0-7618-4439-6 (paperback : alk. paper)
ISBN-10: 0-7618-4439-2 (paperback : alk. paper)
eISBN-13: 978-0-7618-4440-2
eISBN-10: 0-7618-4440-6

∞™ The paper used in this publication meets the minimum
requirements of American National Standard for Information
Sciences—Permanence of Paper for Printed Library Materials,
ANSI Z39.48—1984

DEDICATION

From a Letter written by
Raphael Jacob Moses
Major, Confederate Army
To His Grandson
Stanford E. Moses
USNA – Class of 1892

Sept. 23, 1891

Dear Stanford:

***

And then besides the love of country, you have the pride of Race to battle for. You come from a Race who without a nationality of its own is a great integer in many other nationalities and a source of jealousy and fear in the rest. The apprehension lest they succeed to well (more than religion) is the true source of prejudice.

You can point to your ancestry and show the wisdom of Solomon, the poetry of David, the music of Miriam and the courage of the Maccabees...

***

Your grandfather,
R. J. Moses

Uriah Phillips Levy and Raphael Jacob Moses' ancestry can be traced back to Dr. Samuel Nuibez and a group of passengers who arrived at the Oglethorpe [Savannah] Georgia colony July 11, 1733. Their extended families were very much intermarried over the succeeding generations.

Uriah Phillips Levy
1792–1862

From the Old Testament, 2 Samuel 11:

***

2. Then it happened one evening that David arose from his bed and walked on the roof of the king's house. And from the roof he saw a woman bathing, and the woman was very beautiful to behold.
3. So David sent and inquired about the woman. And someone said, "Is this not Bathsheba, the daughter of Eliam, the wife of Uriah the Hittite?"
4. Then David sent messengers and took her, and she came to him, and he lay with her, for she was cleansed from her impurity, and she returned to her house.
5. And the woman conceived; so she sent and told David, and said, "I am with child."

***

14. In the morning it happened that David wrote a letter to Joab and sent it by the hand of Uriah.
15. And he wrote in the letter, saying, "Set Uriah in the forefront of the hottest battle, and retreat from him, that he may be struck down and die."
16. So it was, while Joab besieged the city, that he assigned Uriah to a place where he knew there were valiant men.
17. Then the men of the city came out and fought with Joab. And some of the people of the servants of David fell; and Uriah the Hittite died also.

***

Uriah Phillips Levy was a United States Naval Officer who served from 1812 to 1862 confronted by a set of circumstances by fellow officers and superiors in the early 19th century as was his namesake "Uriah" sacrificed by his fellow officers and superior as set forth in the Bible.

For he was this same Uriah as was stated in the sworn testimony in this Court of Inquiry.

CONTENTS
URIAH PHILLIPS LEVY
1792 – 1812

Prologue	ix
Part I-Naval Court of Inquiry—1857	1
General Order of Conduct and Appointment to Court	1
Department of Navy	
Extracts of orders, appointments, challenges and authority	
Incident Off Cuba with "Her Catholic Majesties Sloop of War 'Voltaire' in 1823, while in command of Gunboat 158"	3
Court of Inquiry	5
In regard to loss of U. S. Gunboat 158, Uriah Phillips Levy, Lt., U. S. Navy Commander of Gunboat 158 [1823]	
Court Martial #243	6
Charge: "Ungentlemanly and Unofficerlike Conduct"	
Court Martial #324	9
Charge: "Disobedience of Orders"	
Court Martial #330	10
Charge: 1. "Using Provocative and Reproachful Words..."	
Charge 2. "Treating with contempt His Superior..."	
Charge 3. "Scandalous Conduct..."	
Court Martial #389	12
Charge: "Scandalous Conduct"	
Court Martial #454	14
Charge: "Conduct Unbecoming and Officer and a Gentleman"	
Court Martial #795	15
Charge: "Scandalous and Cruel Conduct Unbecoming and Officer and a Gentleman"	
Uriah Phillips Levy—Address to the Court	19
Objections by Uriah Phillips Levy – Extracts of issues, challenges, and objectives to introduction of Naval service records prior to appointment of Captain, USN in 1844.	
Opinion by Judge Advocate	20
Review of Mr. Levy's Objection	
Decision of Judge Advocate	

Part II-Witnesses of the Government 25

General Questions by Judge Advocate 25
Commodore M. C. Perry, USN 25
Commodore S. H. Stringham, USN 28
Commodore C. S. McCaulay, USN 29
Commodore W. B. Shubrick, USN 30
Commodore E. A. F. Lavalette, USN 31
Captain G. I. Vanbrunt, USN 34
Commodore William Mervine, USN 35

PART III-Witnesses on Behalf of Uriah Phillips Levy 37

Recall of Commodore William Mervine, USN 37
Recall of Commodore Charles Stewart, USN 39
Commodore Isaac Mayo, USN 45
Commodore P. F. Voorhees, USN 47
General Questions by Mr. Levy 47
Lt. Peter Turner, USN 48
Lt. Edmund Lanier, USN 53
Captain William J. McCluney, USN 59
Mr. Joshua I. Cohen 60
Lt. John N. Maffitt, USN 61
Dr. William Jones 70
Captain William L. Hudson 71
B. M. Price, Esq 71
Peter G. Washington, Esq. 72
Captain L. M. Powell, USN 74
David S. Coddington 75
Dr. John B. Blake 76
Richard C. Coxe, Esq 77
John James Abert, Esq. 77
Purser Levi D. Slamon, USN 78
John Q. Etheridge, Esq. 79
Benjamin O. Taylor, Esq. 80
George S. Watkins. Esq. 80
George F. DeLaRoche 81
Captain William Salter, USN 84
Asakel S. Levy, Esq. 85
End of Court Inquiry of Interrogation and Cross-Interrogation of
Witnesses of United States Navy and of Uriah Phillips Levy

Contents

PART IV-Depositions　　　　　　　　　　　　　　　　　　　　87

***

December 2, 1857, Depositions of Witnesses not available during time period Court of Inquiry was in session.

***

Interrogatories – Questions　　　　　　　　　　　　　　　　87

Among the persons of the Department of the Navy who were examined by Depositions include:

...

Captain F. H. Gregory, USN	90
Captain James McIntosh, USN	92
Honorable George Bancroft (fmr) Secretary of the Navy	94
Commodore Thomas Ap Catesby, USN	96

PART V-Mr. President and Gentlemen of the Court　　　　101
　Uriah Phillips Levy Letter

The entire record included 900 pages of handwritten recorded documents and several privately published pamphlets on Naval matters.

Index to Supplemental Information	105
About the Editor	109

[NOTE: Commd=Commodore is a temporary (Flag) rank to Naval Captain in command of a multiple ship squadron. Rank of Admiral created in 1862.]

Prologue

Navy Department
September 13, 1855

Sirs,
The Board of a Naval Officers assembled under the "Act to Promote the Efficiency of the Navy" approved February 28, 1855, having reported you as one of the officers who should in their judgment, be stricken from the rolls of the Navy, and the finding of said Board having been approved by the President, it becomes my duty to inform you that accordingly your name is stricken from the rolls of the Navy.

I am respectfully
Your obedient servant,
I. C. Dobbin

Mr. Uriah P. Levy
Late Captain U.S. Navy, New York

...

St. Marks Place, No. 107
New York
May 8. 1857

Sir,
I have to acknowledge the receipt of your letter of the 10th ult. Awaiting your official notice of the Court of Inquiry before which I am to appear and of the charges against me,

I have the honor to remain,
Very respectfully
Your obedient servant,
U. P. Levy

Hon. Isaac Toucey
Secretary of the Navy

...

Navy Department
June 15, 1857

Sir,
Your letter of the 13th ult has been received. The Department prepares no charges against the parties applying for our investigation under the law of January 16, 1857. But on appearing before a Court of Inquiry an opportunity will be given to you, if you deserve it, to hear the testimony against you before

you introduce any on your part thus affording you a full opportunity to meet any charges against you.

I am Sir
Your obedient servant,
I. Toucey

U. P. Levy, Esq.
New York

EXTRACTS OF DIRECT TESTIMONIALS OF CERTAIN WITNESSES

...

EXTRACT OF TESTIMONY OF COMMODORE ISAAC MAYO, USN

...

(A) "We were together in the service in 1825, on board the "North Carolina."

(Q) "Did anything peculiar occur within your knowledge among the officers of the "North Carolina?" ...

(A) "And the object of some of those [officers] was to keep him out of the Ward Room Mess. I asked them if there was anything against Levy, any reason why he should not be admitted as a Member of the Mess—they said he was a d—d Jew and they would not Mess with him."

...

EXTRACT OF TESTIMONY OF LT. JOHN N. MAFFETT, USN

...

(Q) [By Levy] – Was the Christian Sabbath observed on board the Vandalia while under Capt. Levy's command and by his orders? If so, in what manner?

(A) [Lt. John N. Maffett] – It was observed on board, and by his orders. The crew was mustered. No mechanical labor was allowed to be performed on that day, and often, a chapter or two from the Bible was read—one from the New and one from the Old Testament. This was a subject of comment among the officers, in regard to the reading a chapter from the New Testament and in connection with the supposed religious faith of the Commander.

...

EXTRACT OF INTERROGATORY TESTIMONY
BY
CAPTAIN F. H. GREGORY, USN
CROSS INTERROGATORY

...

"I do know that there were in years past officers in the Navy entertaining strong prejudices against him, which, I believe, still exist. I know also, that he has friends in the service as well able to judge of his merits who estimate him very differently. So far as my information goes in relation to this matter, the prejudices existing against him originated in his being a Jew... I, of my own knowledge, know of nothing concerning Ex-Captain Levy which is calculated to bring discredit upon the Navy."

...

EXTRACT OF INTERROGATORY TESTIMONY
BY
THE HONORABLE GEORGE BANCROFT
FMR. SECRETARY OF THE NAVY
MARCH 18, 1845 – SEPTEMBER 18, 1846

...

(Ans. 2nd Q) The good of the Service, moreover, seemed to require bringing forward officers less advanced in years than most of the Captains; and the law sanctioned that course.

(Ans. 3rd Q) I perceive a strange prejudice in the service, against Captain Levy, which seems to me, in a considerable part attributable to his being of the Jewish persuasion; and while I, as an Executive Officer, had the same liberal views which guides the President and Senate, in commissioning him as a Captain, I always endeavored, in fitting out ships, to have some reference to that harmonious cooperation which is essential to the highest effectiveness.

...

EXTRACT OF DEPOSITION
OF
COMMODORE THOMAS AP CATESBY, USN
INTERROGATORY

...

On the arrival of the Franklin of 74 guns at Syracuse in 1818 ... it was understood that Lt. Levy, a supernumerary on board the Franklin, was to be ordered to the frigate 'United States' then short of her complement of Lieutenants. Whereupon, the *ward-room-mess* without consulting me, determined to remonstrate against Levy's coming aboard...I inquired as to the cause, when I was answered that he was a Jew and not an agreeable person and they did not want to be brought in contact with him...

...

CROSS INTERROGATION
BY
JUDGE ADVOCATE

...

(1st A) To the few clamorous opponents thus made, there may be added, the Pharisees of the Navy, who have of date set themselves up guardians of public and Naval morals, and who profess to think that an Israelite is not to be tolerated in or out of the Navy ...

...

It was this same Uriah Phillips Levy, Captain, USN, who at the conclusion of testimony, addressed the final paragraph of a letter to "THE PRESIDENT AND GENTLEMEN OF THE COURT" that document with these words:

...

"And think not if you once enter on this career, that it can be so limited to the Jew what is my case today. If you yield to this injustice, may tomorrow be that of the Roman Catholic, or the Unitarian, the Presbyterian or the Methodist, the Episcopalian, or the Baptist. There is inborne safeguard that is to be formed in an honest, wholehearted, inflexible support of the service, the just, the impartial guarantee of the Constitution. I have the fullest confidence that you will faithfully adhere to this guarantee; and therefore with like confidence I leave my destiny in your hands."

...

Prophetic words, less than a century later that by World War II became evident in Europe (the Holocaust) and in this Millennium, the religious fanatics of unrestricted terror.

...

**PRIMARY SOURCE MATERIAL
and
ACKNOWLEDGEMENTS**

1. American Jewish Archives, Cincinnati, Ohio

2. Historical Records Section, Royal Navy, United Kingdom

3. National Archives, United States Government, Washington, D.C. Record of Naval Court of Inquiry, No. 3 in case of Uriah P. Levy, late a Captain in the U. S. Navy, Washington, D.C., November A.D. 1857 in 3 Volumes with an Appendix

4. Those who assisted me: Kevin Proffitt, American Jewish Archives, Cincinnati, Ohio, Jan Nelson, Personal Assistant, Chattanooga, TN, Sonia Young, my wife of over 50 years

5. Source of Picture of Uriah P. Levy – American Jewish Historical Society, New York, New York

6. Last Will and Testament of Uriah P. Levy – American Jewish Archives, Cincinnati, Ohio

PART I
NAVAL COURT OF INQUIRY—1857

GENERAL ORDER OF CONDUCT AND APPOINTMENT TO COURT

CREATION OF THE COURT OF INQUIRY

...

To Capt. Lawrence Kearney, U.S.N., Perth Amboy, NC:
"By virtue of the authority contained in the Act for the Better Government of the Navy of the United States, approved April 23rd, 1800, I hereby appoint Captain Lawrence Kearny, President, Captains John T. Newton and George W. Storer; Members and Robert Little, Esq., Judge Advocate, of a Naval Court of Inquiry, which is ordered to convent in the City of Washington on Monday the twentieth day of April, A.D., 1857, or as soon thereafter as practicable, for the purpose of making such investigations as may be directed by the Secretary of the Navy... to amend an act entitled "An Act to Promote the Efficiency of the Navy." Given under my hand (NAVY DEPT SEAL) and the Seal of the Navy Department of the United States this 13th day of April, in the year 1857.
I. Toucey, Secretary of the Navy.

...

The said Captain, L. Kearny, was afterwards detached from the said Court by Order of the Secretary of the Navy – and on the 28th day of July, A.D., 1857, the said Capt. John T. Newton deceased – whereupon the following communication from the Secretary of the Navy was rec'd and read by the Judge Advocate.

...

On the 19th, Sept. 1857, the following communication from the Sect'y of the Navy was received and read by the Judge Advocate, to wit: "Navy Department – Sept. 19, 1857. Sir, you are hereby appointed a Member of the Court of Inquiry of which Comm. George W. Storer is President and you will report to him on Monday next, the 21st inst. for duty accordingly. I am respectfully your obedient servant. Isaac Toucey.
To: Capt. Louis M. Goldsborough, U. S. Navy, Washington, D.C.

...

Thursday, Nov. 12th A.D. 1857
Court met pursuant to adjournment. Present: The President, Members and Judge Advocate. The President produced the following order from the Secretary of the Navy, which was read aloud by the Judge Advocate and is as follows, to wit:

"Navy Department, November 9, 1857. Sir: Uriah P. Levy, a Captain in the Navy, dropped by the operation of the Act of February 28, 1855, having made a written request in conformity with the first Section of the Act of January 16, 1857, entitled "An Act to Promote the Efficiency of the Navy," the Court of Inquiry of which you are President is hereby directed to investigate the physical, mental, professional and moral fitness of the said Uriah P. Levy for the Naval Service and to transmit the record of its proceedings and finding in his case to this Department." I am respectfully your obedient servant. Isaac Toucey.
To: George W. Storer, Pres't Navy, Court of Inquiry, Washington, D.C.

...

The said Uriah P. Levy, being also in attendance, was asked by the Judge Advocate to state whether he had any ground of objection, or cause of challenge to allege against the said Court or against any Member thereof. Whereupon the said U. P. Levy submitted in writing (which was read by the Judge Advocate) his objection, or challenge to Capt. L. M. Goldsborough, as a Member of the Court in his case, upon the ground that said Capt. Goldsborough is junior to him, "and had been promoted to the grade of Captain since, and by means of the action of said board," (meaning the Retiring Board under the Act of 1855).

And thereupon the Court was cleared by direction of the President, to consider of said challenge, and the sufficiency of the grounds thereof whereupon the said Capt. Goldsborough stated to the Court that he would be pleased to be excused from sitting in the case, under the circumstances mentioned in the said writing and retired from the Court; whereupon the President and sitting members of the Court decided that the grounds of objection alleged by the said Levy, against the said Capt. Goldsborough as a Member of the Court in his case, is sufficient; and the Court, thereof, sustained the said objection, or challenge; whereupon the President of the Court (after the Court had been reopened and its decision announced) reported in writing to the Secretary of the Navy, the vacancy, thus occasioned; and thereupon the Court adjourned until tomorrow morning at ten o'clock, A.M.

...

Navy Department, November 14, 1857:
Sir, During the investigation of the case of Uriah P. Levy, Capt. L. M. Goldsborough will be relieved from duty as a Member of the Court of Inquiry of which you are President. Comm. L. Kearny will take your place as President and you will act as a Member of the Court. I am respectfully your obedient servant, Isaac Toucey
To: Comm. George W. Storer

INCIDENT OFF CUBA
WITH SLOOP OF WAR 'VOLTAIRE'

Evidence:

And therefore the Judge Advocate offered in evidence on part of the government, the following dispatch from said Capt. U. P. Levy to the Sect'y of the Navy, to wit.

Barracoe, Cuba,
January 22, 1823
Hon. Smith Thompson

Sir:

From Matanza had the honor to inform you of my intended cruise. I now have the pleasure to acquaint of any arrival this day at Barracoe, where I shall wood and water on my passage up Sandeo at the Keys and destroyed a piratical lookout house and telegraph.

On the night of the 7th ult, fell in with his Catholic Majesty Sloop of War Voltaire, Capt. DeOligoris De Sol Cuetos, who was guilty of the most dastardly conduct, this is a second offence to the kind within 18 months. The following is an extract from my journal and a detail of the facts:

At 8 p.m. discovered a strange sail bearing SW out sweeps and swept under her stern, as I spoke the strange sail and was in the act of giving her our character – which was received by a volley round and grape; which did no damage. I continued to hail and she to fire, until my boat boarded her, during which time stayed athwart her stern, within position shot, she being perfectly unmanageable in consequence of caution – I was prevented by prudence and humanity from returning her fire, which I might have done with great execution and slaughter to her without material hazard to me, as long as it remains calm. This course would have sacrificed many innocent and valuable lives at the shrine of the ignorance and cowardly deportment of a Spanish Capt. – my boat was detained. I hailed the Brig and requested my boat to return, this was refused and reply made, that she would be detained until daylight. In consequence of a slight air the Schr. fanned, say a quarter of a mile from her; the Brig wore around and threw another shot at me. My boat still on board of her, she had then been detained about 3 hours. I made sail and run down to the Brig, during which time I had a light at the main peak and hailed her, informing her again that this was a United States vessel of war and wanted to know what he meant by such dastardly conduct, that we were not to be treated with impunity, if he fired another shot he should abide the dreadful consequence that ensued.

I demanded again my boat and then told him the proper course to ascertain who to send his officer on board, if not satisfied with the account my officer gave him, that I would run in company with him to westward. My ship was bound to the eastward and insist to immediate return of my boat, without delay had declared hostilities against us. I then not know how to act; he replies by inquiring by what authority we were cruising in their seas. We were at peace with all the world, in a few minutes after that he sent my boat with half crew and no officer to the above question replied by sending my Commission, by the Surgeon with a demand of a most exemplary meaning for his dastardly conduct. In about ten minutes the first Lieutenant of that vessel which was his Catholic Majesty Sloop of War, Voltaire, came on board at once and stated that the cause of their firing on me was our very suspicious appearance and conduct sweeping down under her stern at night. Inquiring desires the reason why he did not send a boat aboard to ascertain who we were, he stated he believed us to be a Pirate Privateer and was afraid we would run away with his officer and me. He wanted to know, how I would act in a case of this kind. I replied as factual with him, send my boat on board. I found all his conversation amounted to a mean subterfuge, and finally told him that I demanded from his Captain such an apology as would satisfy my Government, but if I did not receive it, that on my return from this cruise I would stop in Havana and take personal satisfaction from his Captain for his cowardly conduct. The officer told me he would inform the Captain of my demand. I told him I should await his return. I treated him with every attention that his rank and genteel appearance demanded. He left at once and a few minutes afterward my boat and officers returned. I waited some time for the return of the Spanish officer, to my great astonishment the Don pocketed the challenge, made sail and I saw him no more—thus ended my conference.

Vessels of war can wood and water here with great expedition, and the Government, as well as the American merchants, are highly pleased with the appearance of American men of war. This is a most excellent rendezvous for our small vessels such as our Sloops, who are on this station during the sickly season as everything can be obtained on the most reasonable terms—no expense for neither wood or water, and in the memory of the oldest inhabitants, never have been troubles with the fever or any other periodical disease. I finished wooding and watering, and shall sail in the morning with the land breeze for Anaqua, where I am informed there is a Piratical Schooner and Sloop. I experienced very great inconvenience and detention in consequence of the shackled state of my only serviceable boat, having to caulk her every time she is hoisted in or out. I trust you will see the necessity of intrusting me with new boats on my return.

In case my former letter has not come to hand, allow me the liberty of again stating the dimensions of two boats, each 18 feet keel and beam in proportion with a loggerhead in the prow to mount a swivel.

Very respectfully,
Your most Obedient Servant
(Signed) Lt. Comdg. U. P. Levy

COURT OF INQUIRY
IN REGARDS TO
LOSS OF GUN BOAT 158

And therefore the Judge Advocate offered in evidence the Report of a Court of Inquiry convened on board the U.S. Frigate Gurrier, at the Navy Yard, Gosport, VA on the 17th June 1823, by order of Hon. Smith Thompson, Secretary of the Navy, and directed by said Sect'y to enquire minutely into the conduct of Uriah P. Levy, Esq., a Lieutenant, in the Navy of the U. States by commander of the U. S. Gun Boat No. 158, in relation to an attack made on that vessel in December last by his Catholic Majesty's Sloop of War Voltaire, and also to enquire into the causes which led to the loss of the U. S. Gun Boat No. 158 in the month of February last, under the command of the said Uriah P. Levy and to investigate thoroughly all the circumstances connected with the case.

Report: Upon a summary of the evidence in their investigation of the conduct of Uriah P. Levy, Esq., a Lieutenant in the Navy of the U. S. lately commander of the U. S. Gun Boat No. 158, in relation to an attack made on that vessel in December, last by his Catholic Majesty's Sloop of War Voltaire, it appears to the Court.

That the aforesaid vessel, on the night of the 7th January last past, while on the north side of the Island of Cuba, proceeding towards Guajava, did fall in with H. C. M. Brig Voltaire, that while at quarters, with every preparation for battle, she was fired into by the aforesaid brig – that after the first fire from that vessel, a boat with an officer was dispatched by Lt. Levy for the purpose of ascertaining the character of the Brig and the causes of his firing into the vessel under his command – that while the boat was on her way towards the Brig, a shot from that vessel was fired, passing over the boat and Gun Boat, No. 158 – that the said boat was detained on board the Brig a considerable time, notwithstanding the repeated demands for her return on the part of Lt. Levy – that when she did return, she was without her officer and part of her crew and bringing a verbal demand from the Commander of the Spanish Brig through one of her crew that Lt. Levy should send on board his papers and authority for cruising in those seas – that after this Lt. Levy did send on board acting Surgeon Smith with his commission, directing him to demand a written apology for the outrage committed on the flag of the United States. That soon after the arrival of the latter officer on board the Voltaire, an officer came from that vessel with a verbal apology from her commander – upon his return to the Voltaire, and not till then, the boat of Gun Boat No. 158, returned to that vessel with her officer and crew. It appears to the Court that there were other shots fired from the Voltaire besides those before mentioned; and that Lt. Levy did not, at any time, return the fire of that vessel – that during the greater part of the time the two vessels were in company, owing to the lightening of the breeze, his position was such as to enable him to engage that vessel with every probability of advantage. It further appears to the

Court that Lt. Levy was at this time in pursuit of piratical vessels, that he was at the very point at which they might have been expected; and that he had every reason to suppose the character of this vessel to be of that nature.

It appears to the Court that neither of the vessels had their ensigns flying during the whole period of the encounter. It appears to the Court, nevertheless, that from the evidence that the conduct of Lt. Uriah P. Levy was throughout the affair, cool and collected and in no respect manifesting a want of personal courage.

With regard to the latter clause of the inquiry, it appears to the Court that Lt. Levy was on his return to the Belize, in Gun Boat No. 158, from a long but unsuccessful pursuit of the pirate LaFitte, that he had on board a pilot refuted to be of unquestionable skill, that on the night of the 12th of February last past, in Lat. 17 deg. 15' N. Long. 88 deg. 301 W (from Greenwich) in the Bay of Honduras, Musquito Coast, the aforesaid Gun Boat No. 158, then under the command of the said Lt. Uriah P. Levy, struck upon a reef between Water Key and Rendezvous Key that the night was clear, and no danger visible that lookouts were kept, and sail shortened. From the facts set forth in relation to the first case of this inquiry the Court are of opinion.

That the attack made by the Spanish Sloop of War Voltaire the United States Gun Boat No. 158, then under the command of Lt. Uriah P. Levy, was most wanton and outrageous; that I was not repelled as it ought to have been, that the sending a boat on board the Voltaire, under the then existing circumstances was highly indiscreet, and that the sending his commission on board the said vessel, on demand from her Commander, was degrading the command confided to Lt. Levy by his government.

The Court are further of opinion that the loss of Gun Boat No. 158, under the command of Lt. Uriah P. Levy, on the night of the 12th February last past, is ascribable to a greater degree of confidence in the pilot than is warrantable in any case, but that after the vessel was actually ashore, Lt. Levy, his officers and crew, with the exception of Wm. Thompson, Seaman, John Thorpe, Seaman and Supernumerary and one other, whose name is unknown to this Court, did their utmost to rescue and preserve the public property from destruction.
J. D. Elliott, Pres't. Walt. F. Jones, Judge Advocate

COURT MARTIAL NO. 243

And therefore the Judge Advocate, officers in evidence, the charges, specifications, finding and Sentence of "Court Martial No. 243 in case of said U. P. Levy, as follows, to wit:

Charge: UNGENTLEMANLY AND UNOFFICERLIKE CONDUCT
Specification: That on Sunday morning the 21st day of July, 1816, in the war room of the U. S. Ship Franklin, Sailing Master Levy ordered the boys to clear away the table for breakfast. That Lieut. Bond said to Mr. Levy that he has no business to give any order whatever without his permission respecting the table being set, that Mr. Levy answered it was not for breakfast, but that they should clear off the table in reply to which, Lieut. Bond called him a damned liar, which words were retorted by Mr. Levy, and such expressions were repeated. That Lt. Bond afterwards observed to Sailing Master Levy that Commodore Murray's letter should not screen him and at the same time challenged him to give any order to the boys that he might have an opportunity of countermanding it. To which the prisoner pleaded not guilty and the Court with the addressed issue to the trial of both the accused upon the matters against them. [Lt. Page and Cook of the Franklin, being the only witness summoned on either side, attended and Lt. Cooper being ordered by the Court to withdraw during the examination of the other witnesses.] Lt. Benjamin Page was sworn and deposed as follows: At the time and place alluded to in the specification, Mr. Levy gave orders to the boys to get breakfast – some time after he told the boys to clear the plates off the table. Lt. Bond said to Mr. Levy, I will thank you to let the boys alone, you have nothing to do with the mess – I am caterer. Mr. Levy said it was not for breakfast he had ordered the table to be cleared off – that he thought Mr. Bond was presumptuous in dictating what he should do. Mr. Bond contended that he has a right to dictate on that subject. Mr. Levy repeated that he had not said anything about breakfast. Mr. Bond told him it was a lie. Mr. Levy said, what Sir, do you tell me I lie? Mr. Bond said yes, it is a lie. Mr. Levy then said, well Sir, I return you the compliment – your conduct is very ungentlemanly. Mr. Bond said to Mr. Levy, you need not calculate upon Commodore Murray's letter screening you from me. Mr. Levy answered he did not intend it should – Mr. Bond was the Caterer of the Mess. Mr. Bond being asked if he has any questions to put to the witness, and were in the negative.

Do you recollect that Mr. Bond said it was a damned lie?

Answer: I am not certain but I think that expression was used.

Question by the Court: Were the accused in the habit of making use of such language to each other? Answer: I never heard such language used. Were the prisoners on good terms previous to the period mentioned in the charge?

Answer: they were. The witness continued: these events occurred before breakfast. When Mr. Levy wanted the table cleared away, it was before the usual hour of breakfast; the Caterer was generally referred to for meals.

Question by Mr. Levy: Did Mr. Bond challenge me to give an order to the boys?

Answer: Mr. Levy said he would order the boys when he pleased. Mr. Bond making allusions to the mess, said I should like to see you at it – you would look damned foolish – they would not miss you.

Question by Mr. Bond: Did Mr. Levy say that he had as much right to order the boys as to the Mess as he had?

Answer: Mr. Levy said I have as much right to do so as he, Mr. Bond, or any person in the ship, but repeated that he has said nothing about the breakfast.

Question by Mr. Levy: Did I mention to you that it was 9 o'clock, before the circumstances mentioned took place?

Answer: I do not recollect but it was later than I had before supposed.

Lt. Benjamin Cooper of the Navy was then called in, and sworn and deposed as follows: About 8 o'clock in the morning of the day referred to, I was in bed, reading and overheard some conversation between Mr. Levy and Mr. Bond, in the ward room of the Franklin. I paid no particular attention to it until I heard the lie given. I heard Mr. Levy tell the boys to bring in breakfast – in a few minutes after Mr. Levy ordered them to clear off the table. Mr. Bond said he has nothing to do with the breakfast and has no business to give any order of the kind. Mr. Levy said he had not ordered the table cleared off for breakfast. Mr. Bond said it was a damned lie or he was a damned liar. I do not recollect which was the expression. Mr. Levy said he was the same, or would to that effect, and that his conduct was very unlike a gentleman's. Mr. Bond said he should recollect that the Commodore's letter should not screen him from chastisement. Mr. Levy made some reply, the import of which I do not recollect – the letter from Commodore Murray alluded to was understood on board to be a letter to Mr. Levy directing him to take no notice of a challenge which he has received. In answer to questions by the Court, the witness said that Mr. Bond was Caterer of the mess. It was earlier than the usual breakfast hour when this conversation took place. I never heard the lie given before between these officers – they appeared before this to be on good terms. The caterer regulated the mess.

Question by Mr. Levy: Was there any established hour for the meals on board?

Answer: There was not.

Question by Mr. Bond: Was not 8 o'clock an unusual hour for breakfast?

Answer: It was.

Question by Mr. Levy: Did not the officers sometimes give orders for breakfast without consulting the Caterer?

Answer: Not order it.

Finding and sentence in the case of Sailing Master U. P. Levy: "The Court also find Sailing Master Uriah P. Levy of the Navy guilty of the charge and sentence him to be reprimanded by the Honorable, the Secretary of the Navy."

...

COURT MARTIAL NO. 324

And thereupon the Judge Advocate offered in evidence, on part of the Government the following *charges, specifications, finding and sentence* of Court Martial *No. 324* in case of said U. P. Levy: "Charges and specifications of charges preferred by Lt. C. P. McCauley, against Lt. U. P. Levy, both serving on board the United States Ship *United States*."

Charge 1st: DISOBEDIENCE OF ORDERS.
Specification: In this, that the said Lt. U. P. Levy, did on or about the evening of the 8th October 1818 *strike* Joseph Porter, a boatswain mate on board the said ship *United States* being a direct violation of the 14th article of the written instructions of his Commanding Officer, as well as a violation of a part of the 14th article for the better government of the Navy of the United States.

Charge 2nd: CONTEMPT TO HIS SUPERIOR OFFICER.
Specification 1: In that he the said Lt. U. P. Levy, did by striking Joseph Porter, a boatswain's mate at the time states in the specification of the 1st charge, violate the positive and written instructions of his Commanding officer, thereby showing a disregard to them and giving a public example of insubordination in the extreme.

Specification 2nd: In that the said U. P. Levy, did, when called on deck by me to examine into the facts of the above mentioned case, reply to me "that he was not to be called to an account in that way" or words to that effect discovering at the same time much warmth in his words and actions, thereby treating me, his senior officer, with contempt on the quarter deck of the said ship *United States*, the charge and specifications being a violation of a part of the 13th Article for the Better Government of the Navy of the United States.

Charge 3rd: UNOFFICERLIKE CONDUCT.
Specification 1: In that the said Lt. U. P. Levy did at the time stated in the specification of the 1st charge, strike Joseph Porter, a boatswain mate, on board of said ship, contrary to the known regulations then existing on board of her. *Specification 2nd*: In that the said U. P. Levy, at the time stated in the specification of the 1st charge, when sent for by me to make inquiries into the circumstances of the fact did reply to me "he was not to be called to an account in that way" or

words to that effect which was uttered in a warmth and manner highly disrespectful to me, his senior officer.
(Signed) C. S. McCauley

Finding: The court having duly delivered upon all testimony in the case, as well that addressed in support of the charge as that offered in the defence together with the statement of the prisoner, the Court are of opinion that the charges and specifications exhibited by Lt. Charles P. McCauley against Lt. Uriah P. Levy are proven and that said Levy is guilty of Disobedience of Orders, contempt of his superior officer and unofficerlike conduct." Sentence: "That said Levy shall be dismissed from the United States Frigate *United States*, and not allowed to serve on board thereof, and that he shall be publicly reprimanded by the Commander in Chief at such time and place and in such terms and manner as he shall deem meet and proper."

...

COURT MARTIAL NO. 330

And thereupon the Judge Advocate offered in evidence the *charges, specifications, findings and sentence* of Court Martial No. 330 in the case of said U. P. Levy, as follows, to wit: Charges and specifications exhibited by Jonathan Dayton Williamson, a Lieutenant in the Navy, against Uriah P. Levy, a Lieutenant in the Navy and preferred to Commodore Charles Steward. Commanding squadron acting out of the United States.

Charge 1: USING PROVOKING AND REPROACHFUL WORDS, contrary to the 15th article of an Act entitled "An Act for the Better Government of the Navy of the United States."

Specification – For that the said Levy at Messina in the Island of Sicily, on or about the 21st day of January anno domini 1819 did falsely, wickedly and maliciously utter and publish in divers places and in the hearing of diverse persons, officers of the Navy and others, the following false scandalous, opprobrious and slanderous words of and concerning the said Williamson, to wit: "He (meaning the said Williamson) is a coward, scoundrel, poltroon, and no gentleman" or words to that effect, and the said Levy, to give the wider circulation and effect to the said false and malicious slander, went about in taverns on shore and at divers mess tables in the squadron, and deliberately, wickedly, falsely and maliciously did utter and repeat the aforesaid mischievous and slanderous words or words to that effect, of any concerning the said Williamson.

Charge 2nd: TREATING WITH CONTEMPT HIS SUPERIOR being in the execution of his officer, contrary to the 13th article of said Act.

Specification – For that said Williamson, on the said 31st day of January was attached to the frigate *United States*, then lying in the harbor of Messina aforesaid was on duty as officer of the deck of said frigate, and the said Levy being a junior and inferior officer to said Williamson – was attached to the same ship, but off duty and under an arrest awaiting the sentence of a Court Martial and the said Levy requested the said Williamson to have a boat manned for him, but before this could be done the said Levy came on deck and without notice or permission of said Williamson went over the side for the purpose of going into a boat that was alongside said ship and manned, not for said Levy but some other, the business and duty of said ship and the said Williamson told the said Levy that said boat was not manned for him but for another purpose, and the said Levy then and there in a rude and disrespectful manner replied "you reported the boat ready for me" which said Williamson denies and the said Levy rejoined in the same rude and disrespectful manner "any boy said you did," which assertion, the boy alluded to by said Levy contradicts and the said Levy replies to the said boy, "you did, you lie you dammed rascal" or words to that effect.

Charge 3rd: SCANDALOUS CONDUCT LEADING TO THE DESTRUCTION OF GOOD MORALS contrary to the 3rd Article of said Act.
Specification 1: For that said Levy, at Messina aforesaid, on said 21st day of January upon the quarter deck of said frigate in the hearing and presence of enemy officers and ship's company of said frigate, asserted that said Williamson has reported a boat ready, when in fact no such report has been made, and that his boy made such a report, when in fact his boy made such a report, when in fact the boy had made no such report, showing and betraying therein a shameful and abandoned disregard of truth, and teaching others who choose to learn from his example, to make use of falsehood and ad easy convenience.
Specification 2nd: For that said Levy is addicted to the vice of lying.
Signed J. D. Williamson

Finding – The Court say that the said Uriah P. Levy is guilty of using provoking and reproachful words and alleges in the first charges of treating with contempt his superior, being in the execution of his office and scandalous conduct leading to the destruction of good morals as alleged in the first, second and third charges exhibited against him by Lt. Jonathan Dayton Williamson as heretofore set forth:

Sentence – "And the Court having considered of the offences of the said Uriah P. Levy under all the circumstances as proved against him, do adjudge that the said Uriah P. Levy be cashiered out of the Naval service of the United States and that this sentence be carried into full and complete effect as soon as may be after the same shall be approved of by the President of the United States."

Endorsement by the President of the United States: Although Lt. Levy's conduct merited consure, it is considered that his long suspension from service, had been a sufficient punishment for his offence; the sentence of the Court is therefore disapproved and he is restored to duty." Signed, James Monroe, Jan. 12, 1821

Names of officers composing the Court: T. McDonough, President; Wm. N. Crane, Jos. Smith, Henry E. Ballard, Wm. L. Gordon, I. D. Nicholson, John Gallagher, Ben F. Bowman, Judge Advocate.

Re-consideration: And now the Court was cleared at the instance of a member and it was moved and seconded that the judgment and sentence in the case of Lt. Uriah P. Levy be reconsidered and the Court having considered of the motion resolved to reconsider as moved – and upon re-consideration thereof the Court say that the judgment aforesaid shall be amended by adding thereunto the following words viz: the Court are of the opinion that all the charges exhibited by Lt. Williamson against Lt. Levy are proved, but lest an injury in the public opinion may be done him which is not intended, the Court find that although instances of falsehood have been proved none have been made out of sufficient importance or malignity to entertain the second specification under the third charge, that said Levy is addicted to the vice of lying."

And upon reconsideration of the sentence aforesaid, the Court adjudge that the same shall stand as at first ordered." (Proceedings signed by the officers composing the Court. January 12th, 1819.)

...

COURT MARTIAL NO. 389

And thereupon the Judge Advocate offered in evidence, the 1st charge and 1st, 2nd and 3rd specifications, together with the finding, sentence of Court Martial No. 389, in case of said Capt. (then Lieut.), U. P. Levy, as follows, to wit:

Charge 1st: SCANDALOUS CONDUCT
Specification 1st: For that the said Lieut. Levy on or about the 8th day of June last (1821) on board the U. S. Brig Spark, on the quarterdeck of said Brig, and in presence of acting Sailing Master Shute, did utter language and opprobrious exhibits touching the reputation of Lieut. Wm. A. Weaver, of the U. S. Navy (to wit) that he, the said Weaver was a coward, a damned rascal, a scoundrel and no gentleman, no one of which assertions the character of said Weaver warranted him in uttering, but all of which was calculated and intended to injure the said Weaver.

Specification 2nd. For that after the 8th day of June last, in frequent conversation below, in the ward room of the U. S. Brig Spark, he, the said Levy, did defame and shamefully abuse the said Weaver in presence of the ward room mess of the Spark, and there did frequently declare that the said Weaver was a coward, a scoundrel, a damned rascal and no gentlemen, thereby laboring to impress on the minds of his hearers that said Weaver was what he represented, all of which was false and without foundation.

Specification 3ʳᵈ: For that the said Lt. Levy, on or about the 8ᵗʰ day of June last, and frequently afterwards, on board of the said Brig Spark, did produce, read and suffer others to read, a note purporting to be a challenge to the said Lt. Weaver and which note, he, the said levy stated he had sent to the said Weaver while at Washington, last winter, and which invitation to a personal encounter, the said Weaver would not accept, all of which was without foundation and utterly false, but which falsehood was calculated and intended to produce an unfavorable opinion of the personal courage of the said Weaver, and that, by the basest of all means, a lie, no such note having ever been received, or heard of until information to that effect was given to the said Weaver by the officer of the Spark, acting Sailing Master Shute, on the 13th day of August, 1821."

Charge 2ⁿᵈ: USING PROVOKING AND REPROACHFUL WORDS, GESTURES AND NUANCES
Specification 1ˢᵗ: "For that the said Uriah P. Levy on the deck of the U. S. Brig Spark, and afterwards in the ward room and before the officers of the aforementioned Brig Spark, did declare the said Lt. Weaver was a coward, a scoundrel, a damned rascal, and no gentleman, accompanied with the apersion [openness] that the said Weaver had refused to fight him, all of which was courtesy to the Act for the Better Government of the Navy."

Specification 2ⁿᵈ – For that the said Uriah P. Levy which of board the U. S. Brig Spark, did say and declare that if the Sect'y of the Navy ordered him to such a rascally mess as the Franklin 74 had last cruise in the Mediterranean, he would apply to the Secty of the Navy for permission to wear his pistols round his neck and he, the said Levy did further state that he would rather fight any Lieutenant in the Navy that ranked him than eat, thereby evincing a quarrelsome and turbulent disposition and injuring the service by such public declarations, contrary to the Act for the Better Government of the Navy."

Charge 3ʳᵈ: UNGENTLEMANLY CONDUCT
Specification: "For that the said Uriah P. Levy did by bad and infamous falsehood and by the production of false papers, endeavor to make it appear to the officers of the Spark and others, that the said Lt. Weaver had refused to accept a written challenge from him, the said Levy, for the nonacceptance of which, he, the said Weaver, was branded and denounced by the said Levy as a coward, a scoundrel and no gentleman – when no such note, in fact, did ever pass and of which the said Weaver was ignorant until informed of his, the said Levy's statement by an officer of the Spark, on the 13ᵗʰ of August, 1821."

Charge 4ᵗʰ: FORGERY AND FALSIFICATION
Specification: "For that the said Uriah P. Levy did forge and invent, for his own wicked purposes, a note purporting to be a challenge to the aforementioned Lt. Weaver and which he, the said Levy, stated he had sent and which the said

Weaver had refused to accept with the malicious and infernal design of injuring or destroying the reputation and character of the said Lt. Weaver."
Signed, William A. Weaver

Finding and Sentence of the Court: "That the first and second specifications, and the facts charged in the third specification of the first charge, except so much thereof as alleges that "he did suffer others" (then acting Sailing Master Shute) to read a not purporting to be a challenge and stating that he had sent the same, were proved by the evidence, and did adjudge him, the said Lt. Uriah P. Levy, guilty of the said first charge of "Scandalous Conduct," but acquitted him of the 1st, 2nd, 3rd and 4th charges. "And the Court, taking into consideration the great provocation given on the part of Lt. Weaver, the prosecutor which had to the conduct of the prisoner, did thereupon only sentence him to be publicly reprimanded by the Commanding Naval officer of this station. The Court, in this sentence, cannot, however, forebear expressing their disapprobation of the behavior of the prosecutor towards the prisoner in so far as the circumstances thereof have come before them in evidence."

Signed, John Shaw, President, Ino H. Elton, W. B. Shubrick, Newton Webster, Wm. Albert, M. W. Wyman, Wm. Aylwin, W. M. Caldwell, Judge Advocate. Approved, September 21, 1821. Smith Thompson

...
COURT MARTIAL NO. 454

And therefore the Judge Advocate offered in evidence the *Charge*, the 1st three *Specifications, finding, sentence and approval of Court Martial No. 454*, in case of said Capt (then Lt.) U. P. Levy, convened at the Navy Yard in Philadelphia on the 1st of November, 1827, by virtue of a warrant from the Sect'y of the Navy, dated Oct. 16, 1827.

Charge. CONDUCT UNBECOMING AN OFFICER AND A GENTLEMAN
Specification 1st (3rd) : That the said Lt. Uriah P. Levy did, on the 19th day of June, in the year 1826, use towards Lt. Wm. A. Spencer of the Navy aforesaid, provoking and reproachful words.
Specification 2nd: That the said Lt. Uriah P. Levy, on the 7th day of June, in the year (page 39) 1826
Specification 3rd: That U. Levy invited D. H. Spencer to fight a duel.
Specification 4th: That U. Levy, on board the U. S. Ship Cyane, did receive and appropriate to his own use, a quantity of mahogany, the property of the U. S.
Specification 5th: That U. Levy did order and direct one Robert Richardson, then on the sick list of said Ship Cyane, to go on shore and perform some work for him, the said Levy's own use and benefit.

1826 on the quarterdeck of the U. S. Ship Cyane, did use provoking and reproachful words to Lt. Frank Ellery, also of the said Navy, and did then and there offer to waive his rank and fight a duel with the said Lt. Ellery.

Specification 3rd: That the said Lt. Uriah P. Levy, on the 19th day of June in the year 1826, did in the presence and hearing of many of the officers and crew of the U. S. Ship Cyane, invite the said Lt. Wm. A. Spencer to fight a duel.

Finding and Sentence of the Court: After maturely deliberating upon the charges, the evidence and the defence, the Court is of opinion, and does pronounce and declare that the first specification is so far proved as that the accused used *provoking* words, not proved as to the reproachful words.

That the 2nd Specification is so far proved as that the accused did, at the time and place specified, offer to waive rank and the residue of the specification is not proved.

That the 3rd specification is proved with the exception of the crew. (That the 4th and 5th are not proved.) The Court is of opinion, and does therefore adjudge and declare that the accused is guilty of so much of the charge as sets forth that the conduct of the accused was unbecoming an officer and not guilty of the residue.

The Court does, therefore sentence and adjudge that the accused be reprimanded by the Secretary of the Navy and that the sentence and reprimand be read publicly on the quarterdeck of every vessel in the Navy in commission, and at every Navy Yard in the United States. The Court feels it necessary to state that the sentence thus awarded to the accused for the offences of which he is convicted, in particular, for giving a public challenge on ship board to another officer, and for offering to waive rank with a junior officer in a controversy arising out of points of duty (offences which the Court deems highly objectionable and detrimental to the service) has been rendered thus mild in consequence of the extent of the provocation to be found in the highly improper conduct of Lts. Spencer and Ellery, which the Court cannot consent to pass over without this marked expression of its disapprobation.
Signed, Wm. Bainbridge, C. Morris, Ino Orde Creighton, S. Cafsin, James A. Renshaw, Alex Wadsworth, Harry E. Ballard, W. B. Shubrick, D. Conner.

Richard S. Coxe, Judge Advocate, November 19th, 1827. Approval, Navy Department, 27 Nov. 1827, Approved. Signed, Samuel L. Southard

COURT MARTIAL NO. 795

The charges in Court Martial No. 795 were preferred by the Sect'y of the Navy upon information of George Mason, a Lt. in the U. S. Navy.

And thereupon the Judge Advocate offered in evidence on part of the Government the first charge and specification, together with the finding, and sentence thereon and approval thereof, of Court Martial No. 795, in case of said Capt. (then Commander) U. P. Levy, and the reconsideration thereof by the Court, in pursuance of the order of President Tyler, with the finding, sentence, be upon such reconsideration, as follows, to wit:

Charge 1st: SCANDALOUS AND CRUEL CONDUCT, UNBECOMING AN OFFICER AND A GENTLEMAN
Specification: In this, that the said Commander Uriah P. Levy, being then in command of the United States ShipVandalia, did on or about the 7th day of July, 1839, cause John Thompson, a boy serving on board said Ship Vandalia, to be seized to a gun, his trousers to be let down and a quantity of tar to be applied to his naked skin. Such punishment – being highly scandalous, and unbecoming the dignity of an officer to inflict and in violation of the 3rd Article of the 1st session of the Act of Congress for the Better Government of the Navy of the United States. Approved 13th April 1800.

Finding and Sentence of the Court – That the specification of the 1st charge is proven. That of the 1st charge the accused is guilty. The Court having passed upon the charges and specifications proceeded to take into consideration what sentence should be adjudged and after mature deliberation, the Court does adjudge and sentence that Commander Uriah P. Levy be and he is hereby dismissed the navy of the United States.
Signed, Ino B. Nicholson, President, W. C. Bolton, Captain, Dan Turner, Captain, Wm. Keever, Captain, E A. Lafallotte, Captain, I. H. Stringham, Captain. Approval, I respectfully recommend that this sentence be approved. (signed) A P. Upshur

April 28, 1842. The record remanded by President Tyler to the Court, with directions to reconsider the sentence, alleged to be too severe. Decision and sentence of the Court upon reconsideration: "In obedience to the Command of the President of the United States, the Court has reconsidered its Sentence in
the case of Commander Levy. Commander Levy was duly informed by the President of the Court and also by the Department that he was at liberty to offer any additional testimony which he might think proper touching the treatment of the boy Thompson.

Additional testimony was adduced by the accused and the Court listened to it with an anxious desire to discover some extenuating circumstances attending this transaction. In this they have been disappointed. The testimony of the accused conflicting in itself, and contradicted in many essential particulars by the testimony on the part of the government, the Court regret to say furnishes no ground for a change in their opinion as to the extent of Commander Levy's offence.

The Court contend themselves with respectfully referring to the testimony as recorded. The point left for the Court to determine is, whether the punishment awarded by its sentence is disproportioned to the offence charged. The impression of the President –as indicated by his order – has been felt by the Court as imposing on it the duty of devoting to the subject the utmost care and as demanding for it, the most impartial consideration.

They have accordingly reviewed their decision with an earnest desire to do justice. They have confined their attention to the single fact of the treatment of the boy Thompson, and have endeavored to rid their minds of all influences from extraneous sources. They feel they have approached the subject with impartial minds and now respectfully submit the result of their deliberations.

The Court is a military and not a civil tribunal, the Act which they are called upon to try is a military and not a civil offence, the laws which govern their judgment are those which regulate the Naval Service of the United States, and the Court as judges are bound to consider what these laws require for the honor and welfare of that service. In this view of the subject we have considered the offence with which Commander Levy is charged: 1st - with reference to the boy Thompson; 2nd - with reference to his effect on the service and 3rd with reference to Commander Levy himself.

We consider it of no consequence whether the corporal suffering of Thompson was much or little. As a seaman in the service of the United States, he had a perfect right to claim exemption from every punishment except such as allowed by law. The law did not allow this punishment – therefore his rights as a Seaman in the service of the U. S. were violated. This is true of all unauthorized punishments. The Seaman has a just right to complain of every arbitrary punishment as an act of tyranny; but he has a peculiar right to complain where such punishment dishonors and degrades him. Punishment however severe is rarely complained of if it be authorized by law, but an unusual punishment – not authorized by law and calculated to subject him to the ridicule and contempt of his mess mates and associates is always deeply felt, and produces on the mind of its subject feelings of bitterness and dislike against his officer, rather than reform. We cannot imagine any punishment more degrading and more calculated to produce such feelings than that which was inflicted in this instance. It involved not only an indecent exposure of the person of the boy, at the gangway of the ship, but the ignominy which according to the received opinions of our people attaches only to the most disgraceful offences. And here the Court will remark, the assertion of the accused in his defence to the contrary, notwithstanding, that during the whole course of their long service they have never seen a boy or man thus degradingly exposed at the gangway of a ship. In this view of the subject, the punishment was not only unusual but wholly unlawful and at the same time exceedingly cruel.

So far as the service is concerned nothing could be better calculated to injure and dishonor it than the conduct here portrayed. The factor might to be able to regard his Commander as his friend and protector. Fighting under the flag of his country, and wishing her life in her service, he ought to feel that the laws are over him and that his rights are protected wherever her flag is displayed.

The power of a Commander is, for the time-being, all but absolute; the discipline of this service requires it to be such, and properly exercised it ought to be sustained. Hence, the offence if of an officer commanding a national ship, *take then shape and character not simply* from the *wrong done*, the *injury inflicted* but from the power *abused*. And when this power is exercised to gratify private passion, personal antipathy, cruelty or for any other purpose than that of maintaining the discipline of the Service and that in a manner authorized by the law, and the usage and customs of the Service, it ought to be punished promptly and the punishment should be graduated by the trust betrayed as well s the wrong done. No other rule of punishment will protect the sailor and save the discipline of the Service. The Court has not discussed the demerits of this offence in the abstract, but as desiring its most aggravating feature from the wanton abuse of power.

It the Service is to exist and prosper, this introduction into it of systems by officers on their own responsibilities must be put an end to. The officer who introduces them tramples on the rules and regulations of the Service, and substitutes his own arbitrary will for the recognized provisions of law. If this is not arrested the day is not distant when Seamen will avoid our national ships, because Sailors know that if an officer be allowed to substitute his will, the law is practically a nullity and that there is nothing to protect him from the most tyrannical punishment. A safe and wholesome discipline is impossible except in strict obedience to law and in the rightful exercise of lawful authority.

The effect produced by the conduct of Commander Levy upon his crew on the occasion under consideration, was an open insubordination which was only overused by the lash. When a sailor revolts, it is the strongest evidence that some act of outrage or cruelty has been committed, for experience teaches us that they will submit without a measure to just punishment.

The Court consider the principle involved in this case was one of vital importance to the Navy, existence of the Navy; they feel that they would be wanting in their duty to the Service if they did not promptly put upon it their seal of condemnation.

As to Commander Levy himself, he was bound to know the law and yet he openly violated it; he was bound to set an example of decency and propriety in his own personal conduct, and yet he has disregarded both. He was bound to preserve the discipline of his Ship and yet he pursued a course calculated more than any other to destroy it and to produce disorder and excite a mutinous spirit in the Service and to being it into odium and contempt.

We certainly have no desire to visit Commander Levy with undue punishment but at the same time we see no reason why we should treat him with under clemency.

We therefore, upon full and impartial reconsideration of our sentence, submit these as our reasons for adhering to it. And do adjudge and sentence Commander Levy to be dismissed from the Naval Service of the United States. Signed, Ino B. Nicholson, Prest. W. C. Bolton, Captain, Dan Turner, Captain, I. M. Keever, Captain, E. A. F. Lafalette, Captain, S. H. Stringham, Captain, C. H. Winder, Judge Advocate. Approval – I respectfully recommend that this sentence be approved. Signed A. P. Upshur

The Counsel of the said Uriah P. Levy objected to all of the foregoing evidence offered by the Judge Advocate and desired that the Court would allow him until noon of Monday next to prepare the said Levy's objection thereto; whereupon the Court adjourned until Monday next at 12 o'clock, m.

Monday, Nov 16 A.D., 1857
Court met pursuant to adjournment. Present: the President, Member, Judge Advocate, Mr. Levy and his counsel. On motion of the Judge Advocate, the reading of the record of Saturday's proceedings was dispensed with, the same having been compared as read; I therefore, the said levy, by his counsel, submitted the following objection, to wit:

URIAH PHILLIPS LEVY – ADDRESS TO THE COURT

...

Mr. President and Gentlemen of the Court: I object to the unacceptability on evidence against me, on this investigation, of the proceedings of the Court Martial referred to by the Judge Advocate in his office just made and of my letter of the 11th of January 1823 and the proceedings of the Court of Inquiry relating to the matter referred to in that letter; and I hereby protest against the reception of each and every part thereof, by this Court, as wholly incompetent and illegal.

...

That I remained in the service from 1823, when the Court of Inquiry was held, until 1855, and that in the meantime I was twice promoted by the action of the President and the Senate, first, in 1837, to the grade of Commander, and afterwards, in 1844, to that of Captain. There promotions are records of the highest character and solemnity.

...

To permit these proceedings to be now dug up from the grave in which they have so long slept, and to be spread upon the record of this Court, as if they have against me on the subject of the present investigations, would be not merely to lumber up the records with useless and irrelevant matters, but to convert that which, in 1823, by the Execution of that day, was deemed innocent or trivial, into evidence of physical, mental, professional and moral unfitting in 1857.

...

The Judge Advocate offers in evidence the charges, specifications and judgments of several Courts martial, held between the years 1816 and 1842, both inclusive, as found in the records of the proceedings of said Courts, filed in the Navy Department. To this I object that such evidence is incompetent and illegal.

...

And because they related, not to my conduct as a Captain, but exclusively to my conduct in the inferior grades of Commander, Lieutenant and Sailing Master.

...

I therefore protest against the introduction of the charges, specifications and findings of the several Courts Martial offered by the Judge Advocate, as evidence to show the truth of those charges.

Again, if this evidence is offered to deprive me of a right which, but for it, I would be entitled to, to with restoration to my rank in the service, and if not offered for this purpose it is objectionable as irrelevant, then I protest against it as intended to subject me twice to punishment for the same offence. These judgments whatever they are have been executed; their penalties have been suffered. Since the infliction of the last of these penalties, and long since those which preceded it, the President and Senate have regarded me as worthy of promotion, and to subject me now to loss of rank for anything therein contained, would be contrary to justice; in opposition to law; and in palpable violation of the principles of the Constitution ... Uriah P. Levy

Tuesday, November 17th A.D. 1857

Court met pursuant to adjournment. Present: the President, Member, Judge Advocate, Mr. Levy and his counsel. Therefore the Court was cleared to consider of the *objection* submitted on yesterday to the evidence offered by the Judge Advocate, whereupon the Judge advocate submitted to the Court the following opinion upon the objection aforesaid.

Opinion by Judge Advocate: Being, *ex-officio*, the adviser of the Court upon all legal questions arising in the prosecution of the investigations before it, it becomes my duty respectfully to submit the following remarks upon the questions now under consideration.

I can not admit that an express enactment of Congress is necessary to make any fact or thing evidence in a Court of Inquiry which is relevant to the subject matter of such inquiry. The fact that such matter of thing *is* relevant, obviates the necessity for any special law declaring it competent. If the law were otherwise, there could be *no* evidence received in such courts, for there is not statute which declares what shall, or shall not be receive as evidence therein. Nor can I admit, that, "unless the records offered in evidence would be legal evidence in civil courts, they can not be so here. This Court is constituted for a special purpose, and its duty is most clearly defined, while in the civil courts, this inquiry could by no possibility arise in its present form.

In January of the present year a law was made under which it becomes the duty of this Court in inquire into, and report its opinion upon, the mental, moral, physical and professional fitness of Uriah P. Levy "for the Naval Service" and in the prosecution of this inquiry, no limit is prescribed other than "the laws and regulations which govern Courts of Inquiry." In Courts of this description there is no special pleading and in the practice therein, no mere technicalities. They have no power to pronounce judgment nor to inflict punishment. Their duties are simply to ascertain and report their opinion upon certain facts, which opinion so reported, amounts to a mere recommendation and nothing more. For what ensues such report, they are in no way responsible. In applying to the proceedings in these courts the rules governing the practice in courts difficulty constituted and professing greater powers, there is great danger of error. There are certain general rules of evidence, like those cited by the learned counsel in the foregoing objection, which are alike applicable to the proceedings and practice in all courts. Beyond these, Courts of Inquiry have little in common with any other description of court whatever.

The construction of the law in pursuance of which this Court has been instituted must be the same as if it were made solely with a view to this case, and as if the name of Mr. Levy were set forth therein as the party whose fitness for the service was to be investigated. No words could have been employed to make the scope of the inquiry broader than it is. What is and what is not competent evidence is a court constituted for such purpose must depend mainly upon its relevancy to the subject matter of the inquiry. Whatever tends to enlighten the Court upon this question of fitness in either or any of the requisites necessary to constitute complete fitness for the Service, must, therefore, be competent evidence in the case, unless there is some rule or provision in the laws and regulations which govern Courts of Inquiry, which would exclude it. No such rule or provision has been brought to the attention of the Court. If then, the records offered in evidence are relevant to the subject matter of the inquiry, they should be received as evidence in the case. Are they relevant? They constitute a part (and probably the only *written* portion) of the history of the applicant's Naval career. It surely needs no argument to prove that the fact that a candidate for office, or high rank, either civil or military, has been many times tried and convicted on very grave offences, is one which bears very strongly upon the question of his fitness therefore. Those retired or furloughed officers who have been fortunate enough to escape such charges and convictions have never failed to urge that fact as one reason why they should be restored to the service, and the Courts have very properly given due consideration to the fact thus urged.

It is conceded that the inquiry should be as to the applicants *present* fitness and that with a view to the rank held by him at the time he was dropped from the rolls of the Navy. But how is this fact to be ascertained without enquiring carefully into everything in any wise affecting his past efficiency? And what evidence can be more satisfactory upon this point than that which he has made or caused to be made, of his Naval career, upon the records of the Navy department? The *effect* of this evidence, it is not necessary, nor perhaps proper, now to consider. If it is competent for *any* purpose, it should be received.

There is one other ground of objection which it is proper to notice somewhat more at length. It is alleged that this investigation should not be carried back of the applicant's promotion to the rank of a Captain in the Navy in 1844, because his fitness for such rank is presumed to have been then passed upon by the President and Senate. Suppose such promotion had occurred on the day before the day upon which he was dropped by the operation of the Act of 1855. If such a rule is sound in the one case it must be equally so in the other, and yet, in the case supposed there could be no inquiry at all, or if any, it would from necessity be confined to *one day only* of his Naval career. It seemed incredible that Congress could have contemplated such an absurdity, in directing this investigation into Mr. Levy's fitness for the rank of a Captain in the American Navy.

Admit if you please, that this question was passed upon by the Senate at the time of his promotion. Does it follow that Congress has no power to order it to be again, and more fully investigated, in case the party shall himself *demand* such investigation? If the President and Senate passed upon it then, the Senate, House of Representatives, and President have united in ordering this Court to investigate and pass upon it now. Why did they do this, if satisfied with their own investigation? For Mr. Levy could not well have proved himself inefficient since that time, having performed no service whatever is his present rank.

Congress did not *force* this investigation upon the applicant. It granted it to him as a privilege upon condition that he would request it, in writing, within a given time, but it gave him no power to prescribe its terms, to say to what period of his career it might be carried, and at what point it should stop. The investigation thus granted to him was intended to be full and complete, with a view to the high character and perfect efficiency of the Navy, as well as that of justice to the applicant. The grand object of the law was to afford to the applicant an opportunity to prove his fitness for the service. He alleges such fitness, and therefore the burden of proving it is upon him. If he were confined to the period since his promotion, it would be impossible for him to produce any very satisfactory evidence in support of this allegation, for the reason that he had performed no service during that time. There is nothing whatever in the Act of Congress directing this inquiry from which the Court has a right to infer that it is to limit its investigation to the period since the applicant's promotion. If such had been its intent, it would have been very easy as to have expressed it. It is not expressed, nor is there any clause, provision or language in the act from which it can be implied. On the contrary, from the absence of any such provision, and from the very broad scope given to the inquiry by the language employed, we are bound to presume that it was designed to be as full, complete, and satisfactory as practicable. If this act of Congress is law, the Court is bound by it, and has no right to interpolate provisions of any sort to suit the convenience of our party or another.

The objection that the reception of records of such convictions tends to subject the party to double punishment has been so often considered by this court that I do not deem it necessary to remark upon it. Offences are not considered here with a view to *punishment*, but with a view to moral, mental, physical and professional fitness for a high, honorable and responsible position.

In relation to the claim on part of the applicant that if the aforesaid records are received as evidence by the Court, as *offered*, the said applicant will insist that the whole of each and all of said records shall be received, as well as the *evidence* upon which the said several Courts acted, as the charges, specifications and findings, I deem it only necessary to say that this Court is not a Court of Appeal, having authority to review and pass upon the *correctness* of the proceedings of the said several Courts Martial. The presumption is that they were competent to perform the duties assigned to them. It is not, therefore, for this Court to enquire whether or not they acted upon sufficient evidence, and the evidence before them is therefore inadmissible for any such purpose. If I have omitted any portion of said records which is properly admissible as evidence in this investigation, it will be competent for the applicant to introduce it; and if believed to be competent evidence, it will not be objected to.
R. R. Little, Judge Advocate

Decision: And therefore the Court, having duly considered the said objection on past of the applicant as well as the view thereof taken by the Judge Advocate, are of opinion and do decide that the said records are competent evidence in this investigation, as offered by the Judge Advocate, and thereupon the Court was again opened, and its decision read by the Judge Advocate, by direction of the President.

Part II
WITNESSES OF THE GOVERNMENT

General Questions by Judge Advocate:
1st: How long have you known U. P. Levy? Have you ever served with him, when, where, how long and state you relative positions.
2nd: From such acquaintance with him, state whether his temper and disposition are such as in your judgment, as to promote good order and discipline in the service?
3rd: State whether you have observed him sufficiently to enable you to determine his mot prominent characteristics? If so, what are they?
4th: Do you know what his general reputation is in the Navy, in respect of those qualities of mind, character and temperament, necessary to ensure proper respect for the rank and Commission of a Captain in the Navy? If so, what is it? And thereupon the Judge Advocate called as a witness on part of the government.

Commd. M. C. Perry, USN who was duly sworn and testifies as follows, to wit.
Answer to 1st general question by Judge Advocate. "I have known Mr. Levy since 1824. He was attached to the North Carolina for 3 or 4 months, I think, in that year, as a supernumerary. I was 1st Lt.; that is the only service I have had with him."

Examination of Commd. Perry Continued:
Answer to 2nd general question by Judge Advocate, [Before the witness answered the said question, the said applicant interposed the following]: *Objection*: "I object to and protest against the question just proposed, on the ground that it calls for the opinion and judgment of the witness on certain supposed facts relating to my temper and disposition assumed by the question to be within his knowledge, without calling for the facts themselves – thus making the witness, instead of this Court, the judge as to whether the same are such as to promote good order and discipline or not, whereas the witness should only state the facts within his knowledge, leaving it to the Court to pass its judgment thereon." Signed, U. P. Levy

Whereupon the Court was cleared to consider of the said objections; and upon consideration is of *opinion*, that the view taken thereof by Mr. Attorney General Cushing, in his published opinion, is a full and correct answer to the objection. The Court would add that questions of this character have been put to witnesses in every case before it, upon both sides and hitherto, without objection, at the time of their examination. The point has been once or twice discussed to some extent in the final argument or "defence" but no view of it has been presented to the Court that has served to change its opinion thereon. And thereupon the Court was again opened and its decision read by the Judge Advocate.

Continuation of examination of Commd. Perry.

Answer to 2nd general question, last stated: For the short time I was associated with him, I saw nothing but an indulgence in indiscreet language (by no means offensive to his brother officers) but calculated to prejudice them against him. I don't think my subsequent acquaintance with him has been such as to enable me to form a judgment upon the question.

Answer to the 3rd question: "During the time that he was in that vessel there was nothing particularly remarkable about him except that he was rather impulsive and eccentric in his manners, fond of speaking of himself and his professional acquirements. I have had no other opportunities to judge of him officially." (At this point the applicant offered the following objection or protest, to wit.)

Objection, "For the reasons urged in the objections and protest filed yesterday, I protest and object to any evidence of any transaction, fact or circumstance in my past history or character anterior to the 29th March 1844, the date of my commission as a Captain in the Navy of the United States, and the years by the Navy register of 1855." Signed, U. P. Levy

Answer to 4th Do: (To this question the applicant objects, as follows):
Objection by Mr. Levy: "I object to and protest against this question, as illegal and inadmissible, because, first, the matter to be investigated by the Court is my physical, mental, professional and moral fitness for the Naval service. This, in each of its aspects, is a question of fact to be determined by evidence of facts, and not of general reputation in the Navy. Second, evidence of my general reputation in the Navy, if admissible to rebut evidence of reputation previously given by me, this is stated in all the books on military law and the practice of Courts Martial, as well as the Treatises on the general law of evidence, and is in effect, conceded in the opinion of Attorney General Cushing, which seemed to be relied upon an Authority by this Court. The government has taken the initiative in this case, and this witness is the first called by the government so that there is not pretext in this case for claiming that I have put the question of general reputation in issue."

Signed, U. P. Levy.

And thereupon he Court was cleared to consider of the foregoing objection and upon consideration is of *Opinion*: That the efficiency of a Captain in the Navy must defend, and *may defend very greatly*, upon his character, or general reputation in the Navy. In the trial of a party upon *charges*, either in civil or military courts, the character or general reputation of such party, can not be put in issue *by the government*, because *specific acts, or offences* can not be proved by general reputation. The Court does not admit such evidence with any such view, nor will it give to it any such effect.

The plain intent of the recent Acts of Congress in relation to the Navy, so far as the same may be gathers from the Acts themselves, was to promote its efficiency. To aid in giving full and complete effect to this intent, is the duty of all who have any interest in the honor of our flag; and especially the duty of this Court upon whose action the reputation and efficiency of the Navy may, to a very great extent, depend. The Court is of opinion that the efficiency of the Navy can only be promoted by having regard to the efficiency of its officers. An argument is not deemed necessary to prove that an officer's efficiency must depend, to a greater or less extent, upon his general reputation in the Navy. If his reputation be such that he can not command the respect and esteem of his subordinates, the service itself must suffer the consequences, and share the degradation of the individual. It is plain, therefore, that the reason of the rule which precludes the introduction of evidence of general reputation by and on part of the government, in criminal prosecutions, does not obtain here; and the reason ceasing, the rule itself ceases. And therefore the Court was opened and adjourned until tomorrow morning at 10 o'clock A.M.

Wednesday, November 18, A.D., 1857. Court met pursuant to adjournment. Present: the President, members, Capt. Levy, his counsel and the Judge Advocate. The record of yesterday's proceedings was read by the Judge Advocate and approved.

Continuation of examination of Commd. Perry.
Answer to 4th general question: "From my own knowledge I know nothing of the details of his life except what I have already stated. But from incidents of his professional career which have become matters of public notoriety, and from the fact of his not having been employed for many years by the government in the position to which his grade would entitle him, I am necessarily led to the inevitable conclusion that he had thus been rendered unfitted for the proper performance of the responsible duties of a Captain in the Navy."

To the foregoing answer the applicant interposes the following *objection* to wit: "I object to and protest against the answer of the witness for the following reason: 1st: It is neither in form not substance an answer to the question put to him, instead of testifying to my general reputation in the Navy, as called for by the question, the witness gives his own personal opinion or conclusion in regard to my fitness for the duties of Captain a matter not only not called for but clearly in admissible.

2nd: The witness, while admitting that of his own knowledge, he knows nothing of the details of my life, founds me uncalled for opinion expressed by him in part, on supposed incidents in my professional career, not called for by the question, and which if proper to be put in evidence on this investigation, can only be proved by witnesses to whom they are known.

3rd: The uncalled for opinion of the witness is in part, founded on the omission of the Navy Department, to employ me, a matter as to which the witness cannot be allowed to testify, because the reason thereof, if proper to be given in evidence, can be proved by higher evidence, to wit, that of the Secretaries of the Navy themselves.

For these reasons, I respectfully insist that the whole answer is incompetent and should not be put on the record, and I pray the Courts to decide."
Signed, U. P. Levy

And therefore the Court was cleared and upon consideration of the objective is of *Opinion* – That is by no means follows that an answer of a witness is not evidence, because it may have been given under a misapprehension of the question. A part of said answer was called for by the question. That portion of his answer in which the witness speaks of the omission of the Dept to employ the applicant in the service, does not seem to be at all important, at least in this stage of the investigation, except as being one of the facts upon which the witnesses judgment as expressed by him is based. If this fact is entitled to no weight for such purpose, that is a proper subject for consideration upon the argument of the case, and in the making up of the final report. It affords no reason for the exclusion of the remainder of the answer.

It is a matter of very frequent occurrence that witnesses, from misapprehension, or otherwise, go beyond the question in giving their answer thereto. This sometimes advocates the necessity of putting another question, but is not necessarily a reason for excluding even that portion of the answer which does not seem to be explicitly called for by the question. If the matter so stated to be unimportant, or, as it sometimes happens, irrelevant, the Court so consider it in estimating the effect to be given to the testimony. The objection is, therefore overruled.

Whereupon the Court was re-opened and its decision announced by the Judge Advocate. Thereupon the testimony of said Commd. Perry was read, pronounced correct, and witness dismissed.

And thereupon the Judge Advocate called as a witness on part of the government, Commd. S. H. Stringham, USN, who was duly sworn and testified as follows, to wit. [The applicant by his counsel makes the same objections to the general questions by the Judge Advocate that were made thereto when Commd. Perry was under examination, and the Court decides as before.]

Ans. To 1st general question by Judge Advocate. "I have known Mr. Levy near 40 years. I have served with him. I served with him in 1825 in the Mediterranean and Coast of Africa, in the U. S. Ship Cyane, about three months I think. I was the 1st Lieut., he the 3rd. We were together in the same ship in 1824 some 2 to 3 months; he was then a passenger.

Ans. to 2nd Do. From my acquaintance with him, his temper and disposition are not such, in my judgment, as to promote good order and discipline in the service.

Ans. to 3rd Do. He is very vain and his manner of interfering where 2 or 3 persons were talking together was disagreeable to the persons present, making statements that were not credited, of facts that could not have occurred, or that were not believed to have occurred by the persons to whom such statements were made, as indicated by their remarks to him at the time, calling them "a lie." He was sent home by the Commodore on account of his making himself so disagreeable to the officers. The officer who made use of this expression was an old Sailing Master.

Ans. to 4th Do. His general reputation when employed in the service was that he had difficulty and trouble on board the vessels where he served. I know there was difficulty in the one in which I served with him and that was his reputation as to his service in other vessels. His mind did not seem to be well balanced. I do not know what his reputation is as a seaman. I did not consider him much of a practical seaman."

Testimony read to witness, pronounced correct, and witness dismissed.

And thereupon the Judge Advocate called as a witness on part of the government, Commd. C. S. McCaulay, USN, who was duly sworn and testified as follows, to wit:

Ans. to 1st general question. I think I have known Mr. Levy since 1818. I have served with him. He joined the Frigate U. S. at Syracruse, I think, in February 1818. I was a Lieut. at the time. I think we were together in that vessel about 16 months. He was a Lieut.; I think he joined as the 4th Lieut. We have never served together since that time and we have very rarely met since. We were in the same Squadron together at Brazil, in different vessels.

Ans. to 2nd Do. [The same objection before mentioned is reviewed and to be considered applicable to the said questions, to whomsoever put, the same decision thereon by the Court.]

Ans. "From my acquaintance with him I think his temper and disposition were not at that time such as to promote good order and discipline in the service. To the best of my recollection it was not very long after he joined the ship that he became generally disliked and finally got into some difficulty which resulted in a Court Martial.

Ans. to 3rd Do. I do not know what are his prominent characteristics.

Ans. to 4th Do. I do not know what his general reputation is. Testimony read to witness, pronounced correct and witness dismissed.

And thereupon the Judge Advocate called as a witness on part of the government, Commd. Wm. B. Shubrick, USN, who was duly sworn and testified as follows, to wit:

Ans. to 1st general question. "I have known Mr. Levy but slightly, personally, at any time. We were in the same Squadron together in the Mediterranean, about 40 years ago. Afterwards, in 1821, I was a member of a Court Martial before which he was tried. After that he commanded a Sloop of War (the Vandalia) in a Squadron under my command. This was in 1839. I took command of the Squadron in March, early in that month. He was then absent on a cruise under orders from my predecessor in command. The Vandalia was sent home in October of same year. He made a cruise of 7 or 8 weeks after I took command of the Squadron, on his return he remained with me until sent home. We have had no other service together that I recollect.

Ans. to 2nd Do. From such acquaintance I am of opinion that his temper and disposition are not such as to promote good order and discipline in the service.

Ans. to 3rd Do. I can only judge of his prominent characteristics from what occurred in his command before mentioned. I was obliged to remove the Senior Lieut. from the vessel he commanded in consequence of the constant or frequent bickerings between them, which I can mention as one instance of his incompentency to command. His Midshipmen complained to me of his making them do duty which was not proper for them. I had to put a stop to that. I had no opportunity to judge of his characteristics from personal observation. These things came to my attention officially. On another occasion, a French Frigate arrived in the Harbor of Pensacola while I was in command of said Squadron. Before I could send an officer on board to tender the usual hospitalities, Mr. Levy went on board, in violation of the well-understood rule of the service, and it was a personal disrespect to myself.

On the cruise he made under the orders of Commd. Dallas (my predecessor in that command), Mr. Levy made some appointments which I considered irregular (and so stated to him in a letter). It is due to him to say that I afterwards confirmed them. During the cruise he made under my orders, his duties were performed to my satisfaction, so far as I now recollect.

Ans. to 4th Do. I am constrained to say that his reputation is the Navy is very low.

On reading the testimony to the witness, he states that the service of which the Midshipmen complained to him, was "requiring them to row a boat, while the apprentice boys were in the stern sheets."

Testimony read to witness, pronounced correct, and witness dismissed, whereupon the Court adjourned until tomorrow morning at 10 o'clock, A.M.

Thursday, November 19, A.D. 1857

Court met pursuant to adjournment. Present: the President, members, Judge Advocate, Mr. Levy, and his counsel. The record of yesterday's proceedings was read by the judge Advocate and approved. And thereupon the Judge Advocate called us a witness on part of the government, Commd. E. A. F. Lavalette, USN, who was duly sworn and testified as follows, to wit:

Ans. to 1st general question. I had known Mr. Levy as a Lieut. previous to 1818. In that year I joined the Frigate U. S. in the Harbor of Majorca, Capt. Crane commanding. I was attached to that ship about a year. Whether he remained so long I do not now recollect. He was in the ship, I think, under suspension from duty when I joined the ship. He was a Lieut. I, too, was a Lieut. at that time. We never served together afterwards, nor in the same Squadron.

Ans. to 2nd Do. From my acquaintance with him, I think his temper and disposition were not such as to promote good order and discipline in the service.

Ans. to 3rd Do. I can only judge of his most prominent characteristics from what occurred at that time. I believed him to be quarrelsome, and with that disposition, it rendered him insubordinate.

Ans. to 4th Do. His general reputation in the Navy was, at that time, that he was quarrelsome and insubordinate, and so far as I know, it is so at this time.

Question by Judge Advocate: Was he at any time, or times, within your knowledge, "put to Coventry?" And if so, when and where? [To this question Mr. Levy, by his counsel interposed the following *objection*, to wit:]

Objection: "I object to, and protest against this question as utterly illegal and inadmissible, for the following, among other reasons: 1st: There is no such condition or relation as that of being "put in Coventry" known to the Naval Code as established by law, and therefore, no such general question as that proposed can legally be put by the government. 2nd: If the condition or relation referred to, be one of a social or conventional character, it is still wholly improper to refer to it as if it were known to the Court; because the Court can judicially know nothing of such a condition or relation. The particular facts, if any, within he knowledge of the witness should be indicated in the question, so as to enable me to object, if the same, as called for, be irrelevant, and so as to enable the Court to decide on their relevancy. 3rd: The question, as it stands, is a general invitation to the witness to detail to the Court matters of scandal, which may not only somber up the record with improper matter, but which the Court, when the same shall be stated, may at once perceive to be improper and irrelevant. Signed, U. P. Levy

Whereupon the Court was cleared to consider of the objection, and upon reconsideration is of Opinion: Without deeming it necessary to pass upon the legality of the question as framed by the Judge Advocate, that it is expedient to change its form, as follows, to wit: State whether or not Mr. Levy dined at the same mess table with the other officers of the ward room and what were his social relations with respect to them? Thereupon the Court was re-opened and its opinion announced by the Judge Advocate.

And therefore, the said Levy, by his counsel, interposed the following objection to the question as framed by the Court, to wit:

Objection: I object to and protest against the question in its new form on the ground that the facts inquired of are utterly irrelevant to the subject of investigation now before the Court, my present "physical, mental, professional and moral fitness for the Naval service" can in no wise depend upon, or be affected by the facts inquired of; especially as they occurred if at all, so long back as 1818." Signed, U. P. Levy

Whereupon the Court was again cleared, and upon consideration, the Court is of opinion that the question now under consideration is mot clearly relevant to the present inquiry, yet the Court approves the withdrawal of the same by the Judge Advocate, and the substitution of the following one, to wit: Question: In what estimate was Mr. Levy held by his brother officers at that time, in respect to any of the qualifications, habits, manners or characteristics necessary to render him fit for his position in the service? And state any acts, facts or circumstances within your knowledge, bearing upon this question as to such estimate.

Whereupon the Court was again opened and its opinion announced by the Judge Advocate.

Ans. to foregoing question: During the time I knew him before 1818 circumstances came to my knowledge of an affair in which he was an actor which made a very favorable impression upon me and on my arrival at the Harbor of Majorca in the Frigate Gurrier, the Frigate U. S. in which he was also lying in that harbor.

He called to see me on board the Gurrier and stated to me, having learned, I think, that I was about to join that ship, that his situation on board that ship was an unpleasant one, as none of the officers of the board room mess were on speaking terms with him except Surgeon Kearny. I sympathized with him, and on joining the vessel, found it to be the case. The Surgeon and myself continued on social terms with him for some length of time. During the continuance of the ship in that Harbor a disagreement took place between Lt. Williamson and Mr. Levy, in relation to a boat in which Mr. Levy desired to go on shore. This disagreement induced Mr. Levy, according to his own statement to me, to seek Mr. W. on shore, where he found him as a hotel, and there denounced him in provoking and reproachful words (the terms I don't recollect). His purpose in making this statement to me was to induce me, as I supposed, to approve his conduct, which I did not do, but reproved him for the course he had pursued as, from all the circumstances which came to my knowledge, he was evidently in the wrong. This conduct, with other of which I had no personal knowledge, as it had occurred before I joined the ship, made a very unfavorable impression of Mr. Levy among the other officers of the ship, which impressions was indicated by their avoiding all social intercourse with him.

I can not state what his reputation that was in relation to his fitness for the service in other respects. This reputation in the Navy is now by no means favorable to him. I think the estimate in the Navy of his professional abilities is a low one.

Cross Ex'd by Mr. Levy. What were the facts that made the favorable impression testified to by you?

Ans. It was an affair in which he received 6 or 7 shots, in mortal combat, without returning the fire, remonstrating at every fire with his antagonist. These facts were not within my own knowledge but came to me as a report.

Question by same: You say this came to you as a report, did you have any cause to doubt its truth?

Ans. None at all.

Question by same: Did you enter the service as Sailing Master and did not Mr. Levy also enter the service in the same capacity?

Ans. I did. That is I returned to the Navy as a Sailing Master. I entered the Navy in 1812 but had previously been in the service. I think Mr. Levy also entered as Sailing Master.

Question by same: Did not officers who entered in this capacity have to encounter much prejudice after their promotion as Lieutenants?

Ans. I think there was a good deal of prejudice as to officers who came in that grade. I have seen it evinced on more than one occasion.

Question by same: Was a warrant ever given to one as a Sailing Master if he was not well qualified as a Seaman and Navigator?

Ans. That I can not say, as no examination, I think ever was had to test their abilities.

Question by Judge Advocate. Had you any prejudice against Mr. Levy on account of his coming into the service in that capacity?

Ans. Not the smallest.

Testimony read to witness, pronounced correct and witness dismissed.

...

And thereupon the Judge Advocate called as a witness on part of the government, Capt. G. I. Vanbrunt, USN, who was duly sworn and testified as follows, to wit:

Ans. to 1st general question. I have known Mr. Levy since in 1821. I have served with him for about 6 months in the Brig Spark, under command of Capt. Elton, in the West Indies. In that year I think of about he was 1st Lieut. I think at that time, a Mid'n. We have had no other service together.

Ans. to 2nd Do. His temper and disposition were not such, in my judgment as to promote good order and discipline in the service. He had some difficulty in his leaving the vessel at Charleston, S.C., before the termination of the cruise.

Ans. to 3rd Do. I have had no intercourse with him since that time, except casual meetings and don't feel competent to judge of his characteristics.

Ans. to 4th Do. His general reputation is not good. I answer under all the heads specified in the question. Testimony read to witness, pronounced correct and witness dismissed, whereupon the Court adjourned until tomorrow morning at 10 o'clock A.M.

Friday, November 20, A.D. 1857

Court met pursuant to adjournment. Present: the President, members, Judge Advocate, Mr. Levy and his counsel. The record of yesterday's proceedings was read by the Judge Advocate and approved and thereupon Commd. Lavalette was recalled at his own request, to correct a statement made by him on yesterday, as follows to wit:

"In speaking of the report as to Mr. Levy's having received shots from his antagonist, I would use the word *several* instead of 5 or 6 and would also amend by saying *before* returning the fire, instead of *without* returning it."

Question by Mr. Levy. What were the duties of a Sailing Master on board a Ship of War when you entered the Navy in that capacity?

Ans. The duties of a Sailing Master were the navigation of the ship and the general superintendence of the rigging, stowing the hold and various other duties."

Testimony read, pronounced correct and witness dismissed.

...

And thereupon the Judge Advocate called as a witness on part of the government Commd. Wm. Mervine, USN, who was duly sworn and testified as follows:

Ans. to 1st general question. I have served with him in the years 1824 and 1825 in the Cyane, under command of Commd. Creighton, I should think, 3 or 4 months, the first time, and about 4 months again, some time afterwards. The first time, I think, he joined as a Supernumerary. We were both Lieutenants.

Ans. to 2nd Do. I know nothing to the contrary of his temper and disposition being such as to promote good order and discipline in the service.

Ans. to 4th Do. I don't know what his general reputation is in the Navy.

I have passed him in the street, perhaps, a half dozen times since our service together, but never to have any conversation with him.

At this point, the Counsel of Mr. Levy insisted that the following paper be spread upon the record, to wit:

In answer to the 4th general interrogatory on this part of the government, the witness, after saying, "I don't know what his general reputation in the Navy is," immediately added, and as a part to this answer to the question, "I have heard rumors of petty, trifling matters, but I know nothing of my own knowledge, to his disadvantage as an officer and a gentleman. The Judge Advocate has not recorded these additional words. I respectfully claim and insist that they ought to be recorded as a part of the answer, and I refer to the answers, as recorded, of Commds. Perry and Stringham to the same question of the record to show that in the answers of those witnesses, matters of the like nature, prejudicial to me, forming parts of the answers of those witnesses, were entered upon the record.
I respectfully insist on the same measure of justice to me, in recording the answer of the present witness.

Signed, U. P. Levy

To which the Judge Advocate replied that he "had not objected and does not now object to the recording of any portion of the witnesses answer that is deemed evidence if stated as such; and thereupon repeated the question to the witness.

Continuation of the answer of Commd. Mervine. I have heard rumours of petty, trifling matters, but I know nothing of my own knowledge, to his disadvantage as an officer and a gentleman. I have nothing further to answer to the question.

Cross Examined by Mr. Levy. Who was 1st Lieut. of the Cyane during the time referred to you?

Ans. The present Commd. Stringham.

Question by same: Was there more than one Sailing Master on board the vessel and who was he?

Ans. Only one, Naham Warren was his name.

Question by same: Is he living or dead, and if dead, when did he die?

Ans. He is dead. I do not know when he died.

Testimony read to witness, pronounced correct and witness dismissed.

PART III
WITNESSES ON BEHALF OF URIAH PHILLIPS LEVY

And thereupon, the Judge Advocate, having examined all the witnesses summoned on the part of the government who have reported (except one or two not deemed material) rests for the present, reserving the right to examine Lt. Ausmussen, Ex-Lt. E. C. Anderson and Ex-purser Job Bryan if they, or either of them report before the close of the investigation if he shall think proper to do so.

And thereupon the Counsel for Mr. Levy presented the following paper and desired that the same be placed upon the record. "Before commencing the introduction of evidence on my part, I have to ask that the records of the Court of Inquiry and of the several Courts Martial, whose report, charges, specification and findings were put in evidence by the government, may be placed in the possession of the Court, so that the Court may be enabled to see whether the record in each case is perfect and duly authenticated, and to the end also, that I may be enabled to avail myself of my right to refer to and use such as may be legal parts of the record not put in evidence by the government."

Signed, U. P. Levy

To which the Judge Advocate replied that said records had been in the custody of the Court since first put in evidence, and that he had previously informed the Counsel that they are always accessible whenever required. And thereupon the said Mr. Levy recalled as a witness in his behalf, Commd. Wm. Mervine USN, who testified as follows, to wit:

Question by Mr. Levy. State whether or not, at any time during the cruise of the U. S. Ship Cyane while Capt. Levy was on board of her, you heard Sailing Master Warren say to Capt. Levy, in reference to any statement made by him, that such statement was "a lie"?

Ans. I never heard of it. I will add that I do not recollect ever to have heard the subject mentioned.

Question by same: Could such an incident have occurred and the same not have been heard of by you?

Ans. It is possible. I can't say as to that.

Question by same: Was it in accordance with the general character and disposition, and the usual modes of speech of Sailing Master Warren, as the same were known to you, that he should seriously make to any one, in ordinary conversation, such a remark?

To the foregoing question the Judge Advocate objects because it opens a collateral inquiry and one having no direct bearing upon this investigation. The Judge Advocate adds that he is desirous of avoiding all captions, as merely technical objections and does not insist upon this one as at all important except as consuming time unnecessarily, and lumbering the record with immaterial and irrelevant matter.

The Court, being cleared, is of opinion that the question is entirely unimportant, as an answer thereto, whether affirmative or negative, would neither prove or disprove any fact. The vague inference that might be drawn from such an answer is not such a one as Courts can attach any importance to. If it be competent to *disprove* a fact by such evidence, it would be equally so to *prove* the fact by the same character of evidence with that the person referred to was in the habit of using such expressions, I therefore *did* use the one referred to. No rule of evidence has ever been brought to the attention of the Court under which such a fact could be either proved or disproved by such evidence.

Inasmuch, however, as the objection is not insisted upon as of importance in the inquiry itself, the Court does not object to permit the question to be answered in this instance if insisted on by the applicant, being desirous of conforming, so far as consistent with duty, to views and wishes, in conducting the investigation.

Thereupon the Court was reopened and its decision read by the Judge Advocate.

Answer to foregoing question: I did not regard him as a man of that character, as he was not a man of decision or firmness; I can hardly believe he would make use of such an expression except as a matter of joke, to any one.

Question by same: Was it in accordance with the character, disposition and habits of Capt. Levy, as then known to you, that such a remark should be seriously made to him, by any one, without its being instantly and decidedly repelled? [The foregoing question was objected to as before, being open to the same objection as the one immediately preceding and it was decided by the Court as before.]

Ans. I think not. I only speak from his general character from which I think he would not be apt to tolerate such an insult.

Testimony read to witness, pronounced correct and witness dismissed. And thereupon the said Mr. Levy offered in evidence his "protection" under date of August 7, 1804, as an "American Seaman" aged 14 years, or thereabouts, and signed "Tho's Wilson" as D.C.U.S. which was read by the Judge Advocate.

And thereupon the said Levy offered the following paper, which was read in evidence:

"Custom House Philadelphia
Collectors Office, June 26, 1856
I hereby certify that on the 7th day of October, A.D., 1811, there was issued from the Custom House at the Port and District of Philadelphia a certificate of enrollment for the Schooner "George Washington," built at Dennis Creek in the State of New Jersey in the year 1811 of the burthen of 138 and 40/95th tons, if that Geo. Mifshent together with Uriah P. Levy of Philadelphia, and Washington Garritson, of the County of Cape May, state of New Jersey, were the true and only owners and that Uriah P. Levy was the Master of said Schooner which cleared at this Port for Teneriffe, October 9, 1811. In witness whereof I have this day and date aforesaid affixes my signature and seal office."
[Seal] Wm. Harbison, Dep. Col.

And thereupon the said Levy called as a witness in his behalf, *Commd. Charles Stewart, USN*, who was duly sworn and testified as follows, to wit:

Question by Mr. Levy. Are you acquainted with Capt. U. P. Levy? If yea, how long have you known him?

Ans. I have known him since 1816.

Question by same: Has he ever served with you, if so, when, where and how long? Please state your relative positions at the time.

Ans. He served under me 18 months or two years, commencing in 1816 in the Franklin 74. I commanded. He was 2nd Sailing Master and promoted by the government to a Lieutenancy while on board of that ship. He served as a Lieut. in that Ship until somewhere about February 1818, when he was transferred to the Frigate U.S., forming one of the Squadron under my command and remained in that ship, I think, until she was sent home and returned in her.

Question by same. During his service on board the U. S. Ship Franklin as 2nd Sailing Master, how did he perform his professional duties?

Ans. To my perfect satisfaction, so far as I learned.

Question by same: State whether or not you recommended him to the Navy Dept for promotion to a Lieutenancy?

Ans. I think I did; and appointed him as the 2nd Sailing Master of the Franklin on the 2nd April 1816, which was confirmed by the Secretary afterwards.

Question by same: Was the paper now shown you marked "A" [not included] the letter of recommendation referred to by you, from yourself to the Dept?

Ans. It is.

Question by same. Do you know the signatures to paper marked "B" [not included] and others now shown you, now shown you, if so are they genuine, and were they officers in the ship?

Ans. I recognize all except the first one, and believe them genuine. They were all officers of the Ship at the time. I am not familiar with the signature of paper marked "C" [not included]. I know the signature to paper marked "D" [not included] and believe it genuine. I also know the signature to paper marked "E" [not included] and believe it genuine. I know that to paper marked "F" [not included] and believe it genuine. I also know that to paper marked "G" [not included] and consider it genuine. I know that to paper marked "H" [not included] and believe it genuine. Charles W. Morgan was 1st Lieut. of the Franklin at the time of the date of paper marked "B" [not included].

And therefore the Court adjourned until tomorrow morning at 10 o'clock A.M.

Saturday, November 21st, A.D. 1857

Court met pursuant to adjournment. Present: the President, members, Judge Advocate, Mr. Levy and his counsel. The record of yesterday's proceedings was read by the Judge Advocate and approved.

And thereupon the said Mr. Levy recalled Commd. Stewart who continued as follows, to wit:

Question by Mr. Levy. During Capt. Levy's service on board the Franklin, as Lieut. how did he perform his professional duties?

Ans. To the satisfaction of the Captain of the ship as well as the other officers, I believe.

Question by same. When did he leave the U. S. Ship Franklin and to what vessel was he transferred?

Ans. He was transferred to the Frigate U. S. some time in February 1818, I think. Capt. Crane commanded that Frigate.

Question by same. Did anything occur in reference to Lt. Levy's reception on board the U. S. Ship U. S. leading to a correspondence between Capt. Crane and yourself? If so, state what it was. State also the unusual nature of the correspondence.

Ans. In distributing to the Squadron officers that were considered supernumerary in the Franklin, (she having more than her complement) Lt. Levy was directed to join the U. S. by an order to Capt. Crane to receive him. In conformity with his orders Lt. Levy reported himself to Capt. Crane and delivered to him my letter to him, directing him to receive him. To the order to Capt. Crane he replied in a note to me that he was surprised that I should force upon him an officer that he had not desired, sending him back again to the Franklin. I then wrote to him that it was painful to me to have to give a second order to remove an officer, that if there were any allegations against Lt. Levy, the law was open to him to put them in the form of charges, and I would at all times be ready to afford him a trial, that I could not permit an officer under my command, bearing the confidence and commission of the government of the U. S. to be thus treated. Lt. Levy was then sent back to the Frigate U. S. where he remained until her return to the U. S. I speak from recollection, as I have not seen the papers for many years. [To the foregoing question and answer the Judge Advocate interposed a general objection on the grounds of issues.]

Question by same. Look at paper now shown to you marked "I" [not included] and state whether or not it was sent by your order at the time of its date to the then Lt. Levy?

Ans. It was written by my authority or direction to Lt. Weaver, and sent to Lt. Levy. Said letter was then given in evidence, and is as follows, to wit:

Letter: Commd. Stewart assures Mr. Levy that the reports existing against him, at the time he applied for an appointment to the Franklin were cleared up by the documents and reasons of Mr. Levy, perfectly to the satisfaction of Commd. Stewart, as well as the government of the U. S. Commd. Stewart also assures Mr. Levy that he had not removed him from the ship under his command in consequence of any objections to his having him in his ship, or in consequence of any reports of his officers, but in conformity with the views of the government, in having the officers attached to the Squadron distributed in such manner as to afford them the best opportunity to acquire experience in the service; the principal object of employing either the ships or officers in the Navy. When an officer is to be removed from one ship to another, the course the Commd. will pursue will be to remove a junior officer, unless the nature of the case should require otherwise. Franklin, February 5, 1818 (a true copy) signed Wm. A. Weaver, Chief Aid to Commander in Chief, U. S. Navy Forces, Mediterranean Sea

Question by same. Look at paper now shown you, marked "J"[not included], state whether or not it is an authentic document and whether or not it was shown to you on, or before, the 5th of February 1818?

Ans. This appears to be authentic, so far as I can judge of it. I think it probable it may have been shown to me the, but have no distinct recollection.

Said letter was then read in evidence and is as follows, to wit:

Letter: Navy Dept, March 29, 1816
Sir, In reply to your letter of the 22nd ult, I inform you that no cause exists in this Dept to justify a compliance with your request. No charges or complains have been made against you, and your character as an officer stands unimpeached. The frivolous reports of ill disposed persons cannot form a sufficient cause of appeal to a tribunal of officers, not can the frequent personal disputes between the officers in service engage the attention of this Department, except in cases of direct violation of the Rules and Regulations for the government of the Navy. You will therefore consider yourself free from reproach and from any prejudice unfavorable to your character as reflects this Department. I am respectfully your obedient servant, B. E. Crowninshield
Mr. Uriah P. Levy, Sailing Master, USN, Philadelphia

Question by Mr. Levy. State whether or not the paper marked "J"[not included] was referred to in your said communication to Lt. Levy of February 5, 1818, where you speak of the views of the government.

Ans. I have no recollection of having had any reference to that paper at all in that action. I referred to the general instructions of the government.

Question by same. What led to your sending your communication of Feb. 5th, 1818, to Lieut. Levy?

Ans. The supposition that he had been transferred from the Franklin on account of some misconduct there. I acted under the impression that it may have been supposed by the officers of the U. S. that he was transferred from such a cause. [At this point the applicant, by his counsel, desired the witness to look upon the last three pages of the record of Court Martial No. 324, reciting a letter from Commd. Stewart, referring the question of approval or disapproval of the proceedings to the President of the U. S. and alleging some informalities, omissions and irregularities therein, not defined or explained in said letter, proposing to ask the witness in regard to the authenticity thereof and to put the same in evidence. The consideration by the Judge Advocate desired that the Court might be cleared with the view of questioning as to the propriety of placing upon this record at length portions of the records of said Courts Martial that be believed to be entirely unimportant.

The Court being cleared, the pages referred to were read to the Court by the Judge Advocate and upon consideration the Court was of opinion that that portion of said record referred to was not of sufficient importance in this investigation, to render it actually necessary or proper, that it should be spread *at length* upon the record were a proper evidence at all. Insomuch as the Judge Advocate

Part III: Witnesses on behalf of Uriah Phillips Levy

forebears to object to the relevancy of the paper and his objection solely upon the necessary of expediency, with a view to time upon the encumbering of the record, the Court and not think it necessary to pass upon this question, being desirous of giving to the officer the benefit of any doubt it may examine in regard to any question arising in the investigation.

To the same records are very voluminous and consist much of matter wholly improper to the consideration of this event. The accused recommends that the substance of this issue now under consideration be entrusted upon the record of the Judge Advocate in the form following, to wit:

And thereupon the said Levy offered in evidence a memorandum, signed by the members of the Court Martial, number 324, at the issue of said record, reciting a letter of the Commd. Stewart referring the question to the approval or disapproval of the proceeding to the President of the United States and alleging upon informalities, answers and omissions and irregularities listed therein, not explained in said letter such was read in evidence. Thus pulling this portion of said record in evidence to reopen whatever consideration it may or entitled to and offering the counsel in opportunity, should they desire it necessary, may be read, to recite the very records of the violations of the period in question in their final argument. The court finds that the cause so recommended is a liberal one, and it desires to pursue no other, and fully approves the suggestion of the Judge Advocate, to waiver all merely technical objections, so far as duty to the service and to the country will permit.

And thereupon the Court was re-opened and by direction of the President the Judge Advocate stated the conclusion and recommendation by the Court.

And thereupon the said Levy, by his Counsel, submitted the following paper, and desired that the same should be recorded in the proceedings.

The Judge Advocate, having given in evidence the record of the proceedings of a Court Martial held November 18, 1818, on board the U. S. Frigate *United States* by order of Commd. Stewart, Commander in Chief, this, before which Court I was tried, and having read in evidence certain charges and specifications on which I was convicted, together with the judgment and sentence of the Court, but not having read in evidence that part of the record which sets forth the disapproval of the proceedings of said Court Martial by said Commander in Chief and his reference of the proceedings to the President of the U. S., I now offer to read in evidence said disapproval as entered on the record, in the following words. U. S. Ship Franklin, Syracuse Harbor, November 24, 1818.

"The Commander in Chief has received and perused the proceedings of the general Court Martial ordered to be held on board the Frigate U. S. on the 18th inst, for the trial of the several offenders as set forth in the warrant dated on the 16th day of the present month. It appears to the Commander in Chief that some omissions, irregularities and informalities have arisen in the course of the proceedings that some parts of the sentences are outré and inconsistent with the spirit and intent of the law enacting rules and regulations for the better government of the Navy, as well as infringing exclusive rights and prerogative tending to embarrass the service without producing a relative good and only calculated to set up an inadmissible precedent. The Commander in Chief of the Squadron after a due exercise of his best judgment thereon and the instructions of the Hon. Secretary of the Navy to him directed, deems it improper to approve (as inconsistent with those instructions and his duties) the proceedings of the Court above referred to, but considers it highly proper that they should be referred to his Excellency, the President of the U. S. and Commander in Chief of the Naval Forces thereof with such remarks as may tend to explain the difficulties of the Commander of the Squadron and to illustrate the proceedings thereon. He believes the decision of the above high authority will be more satisfactory to the Court and beneficial to the service. The Commander in Chief therefore directs that the several prisoners under sentence be released from all unnecessary restraint but remain suspended from duty until the pleasure of the president of the U. S. is made known. The Commander in Chief also directs that the Court desist from further proceedings under the warrant dated on the 16th day of the present month of November 1818, and recommends that the general Court Martial assembled under the above warrant, after reading this be dissolved."

And I propose and claim the right to ask the witness whether or not he received from the President of the U. S. any order or instruction in respect to the proceedings of said Court, so referred to him by the witness of such Commander in Chief. Signed, U. P. Levy

Whereupon the Judge Advocate states that the question so proposed to be put to the witness had not been, and would not be objected to. The Court having already received the paper recited in the foregoing statement in evidence, no new question is raised thereby for the Court's decision, and thereupon the Court adjourned until Monday morning next, at 10 A.M.

Monday, November 23rd, 1857
Court met pursuant to adjournment. Present: the President, members, Judge Advocate, Mr. Levy and his counsel. The record of yesterday's proceedings was read by the Judge Advocate and approved.

And thereupon the said Commd. Stewart was recalled and testified as follows, to wit:

Ans. I received from the Secretary of the Navy a communication approving my proceedings in regard to the cases referred to.

Question by Mr. Levy. From what you have know of Capt. Levy, state whether or not you believe him physically, mentally, professionally and morally competent to perform the duties of a Capt. In the Naval service of the U. S. and fit for said service?

Ans. Certainly I do. I can't think otherwise of him having no knowledge of any deficiency in that respect.

Question by same. If you were in command of a squadron, would you or not be willing to have him as a Commander of one of the ships in your squadron?

Ans. I should have no objection whatever, having full confidence in his skill and seamanship, to giving him command of a ship in the squadron or of my flagship.

Question by same. State whether or not it is important to the highest efficiency of an officer of the Navy that he should understand the use of the oar?

Ans. It would be no disadvantage to him to understand the use of the oar. The use of the oar is a part of the business of a seaman; and the more qualifications he possesses, the better.

Question by same. State whether or not, for the purpose of teaching young Mid's the use of the oar it is in your judgment proper for the for the Commander of a ship to require them, occasionally, to row one of the ships boats?

Ans. It may be the practice with some commanders, but, perhaps, not all. It depends upon what interest they take in the proficiency of the Mid's.

Cross Ex'd by Judge Advocate. Have you ever seen Mr. Levy in command of a ship?

Ans. I have not. He never served under me in command of a ship.

Testimony read to witness, pronounced correct and witness dismissed. And thereupon the said Mr. Levy called as a witness in his behalf, Commd. Isaac Mayo, USN, who was duly sworn and testified as follows, to wit:

Question by Mr. Levy. Are you acquainted with Capt. U. P. Levy? If yea, how long have you known him?

Ans. I am and have known him ever since the War of 1812.

Question by same. Has he ever served with you, if so, when, where and how long? Please state your relative positions at the time?

Ans. We were associated together in the service in 1825 on board the North Carolina. I can't say as to the precise time, I should think about a month. I was Flag Lieut. to Commd. Boyers. He was a Lieut. ordered to take passage in the Ship to the Mediterranean.

Question by same. Did anything peculiar occur within your knowledge among the officers of the North Carolina in relation to his reception on board that ship? If yea, state the same particularly.

Ans. I had returned from recruiting and upon my re-joining the ship (I had been absent for 7 or 8 months), some of the junior officers of the ward room mess asked me if I knew that Levy had been ordered to take passage in the ship, and the object of some of them was to keep him out of the ward room mess. I asked them if there was anything against Levy and reason why he should not be admitted as a Member of the Mess. They said he was a d____d Jew and they would not mess with him to which I answered that if that was all, I should certainly vote for his admission to the Mess. Anyhow, that was the place for him and we had no right to exclude him as he was ordered there by the Secretary of the Navy and I heard no more of it.

Question by same. From what you have known of Capt. Levy, state whether or not you believe him physically, mentally, professionally and morally competent to perform the duties of a Capt in the Naval service of the U.S. and fit for said service?

Ans. I look at him. I should say he is physically and mentally competent. Professionally, I have never heard it doubted. I considered him a good seaman and brave man.

Cross Ex'd by Judge Advocate. Did you ever see him in the performance of his professional duties?

Ans. No. Only from reports.

Question by same. Who were the junior officers of the North Carolina who used the language you mentioned in relation to Mr. Levy's being excluded from the Ward Room Mess?

Ans. Two of them were Marine officers, Carter and Randolph and were very violent in their opposition to his admission to the Mess. I think Lieut. Griffin (the junior Lieut.) was another who opposed it. I think it was Carter, a Marine officer who employed the language, the others assented to it.

Question by Mr. Levy. What was Lieut. Levy's deportment as an officer of the Mess?

Ans. Correct in every respect. He took his meals and generally retired. He was not a general favorite, some of the officers kept themselves aloof from him and he did from them.

Testimony read to witness, pronounced correct and witness dismissed. And thereupon the said Levy called as a witness in his behalf *Commd. P. F. Voorhees, USN*, who was duly sworn and testified as follows, to wit.

Ans. to 1st general question by Mr. Levy. I am acquainted with Mr. Levy and have known him since the early part of 1825, perhaps longer.

Ans. to 2nd Do. He went out as a passenger with me in 1825, in the N.C. from the U. S. to the Mediterranean. I was the 2nd Lieut. of the ship.

Ans. to 3rd Do. My impression was then that he was mentally, morally and physically capable. My impression is the same of him now. Professionally I can not speak, as we did not do duty together. I have no reason to doubt his professional fitness. I found him an agreeable Mess Mate and a gentlemanly officer. I have met him a number of times since, and have always found him gentlemanly and polite.

Question by same. During your intercourse with him did you ever discover any such temper or disposition as was calculated to impair his efficiency, or mar the harmony of the service?

Ans. I have not.

Question by same. If you were in command of a squadron, would you or not be willing to have Capt. Levy as a Commander of one of the ships in your squadron?

Ans. I would.

Cross Ex'd by Judge Advocate. Did you ever serve with Mr. Levy either on shore or afloat, and have you seen him in the performance of duty?

Ans. I have not.

Testimony read to witness, pronounced correct and witness dismissed.

General Questions by Mr. Levy

1st Are you acquainted with U. P. Levy, late a Capt, in the Navy? If yea, how long have you known him?

2ⁿᵈ Has he ever served with you? If yea, when, where and how long and what were your relative positions?

3ʳᵈ From what you have known of him, state whether you believe him **physically, mentally, professionally and morally competent to perform the duties of a Captain in the Navy and fit for said service?**

4ᵗʰ During your intercourse with him, did you ever discover any such temper or disposition as was calculated to impair his efficiency, or mar the harmony of the service?

And thereupon the said Levy called as a witness in his behalf, *Lieut. Peter Turner, USN*, who was duly sworn and testified as follows, to wit:

Ans. to 1ˢᵗ general question by Mr. Levy. I am, and have known him since the latter part of 1824.

Ans. to 2ⁿᵈ Do. He has served with me, in November 1825, in the Cyane, until in July 1827. I was an Acting Mid'n, Mr. Levy was a Lieut. in the latter part of 1824 he came home as a passenger in the Nonesuch. I was with him then about 4 months. We have had no other service together.

Ans. to 3ʳᵈ Do. From my recollection of him I do consider him fit. I consider him very well qualified.

Ans. to 4ᵗʰ Do. During my intercourse with him I did not discover any such temper or disposition as was calculated to impair his efficiency or mar the harmony of the service.

Question by same. Where was the U. S. Ship Cyane when he joined her? Who was his Commander and to what ports did the ship go?

Ans. The Cyane was at the Navy Yard, N. Y. I found him there when I joined her, in temporary command, I think, of the vessel. I think he lived on board or had a part of his things there. Capt. Jesse D. Elliott was her Commander. The vessel went to Pernambuco, St. Salvador, Rio Janerio, Montevideo, Buenos Ayres and Santos and on our return at St. Thomas, St. Bartholomew, Havana and Matamoros, thence to Philadelphia.

Question by same. How did Lt. Levy perform his duties during the cruise of the Cyane?

Ans. Very properly, so far as I can recollect and zealously; apparently to the satisfaction of Capt. Elliott.

Question by same. State whether or not the main mast of the ship was taken out at any time? If so, where was she, and what officer was charged by her commander with the performance of this duty?

Ans. The main mast was taken out of the ship twice, 1st at Rio Janeiro, where we made a new masthead. Mr. Levy, as near as I can recollect, was detailed by the Commander to attend to all unusual and heavy duties. The next time the mast was taken out at Santos and lengthened. Mr. Levy superintended the getting the mast out and superintended the gangs. It was considered a very nice piece of work to lengthen the mast in that way. I was detailed to take charge of one of the gauges on shore and saw Mr. Levy almost every day.

Question by same. Did, or not, the operations you have described as to the Mast require knowledge, experience and skill in seamanship on the part of the officer superintending the same?

Ans. It did.

Question by same. Did they, are not, properly belong to Lieut. Levy or to some other officer? If so, why was the duty imposed on Lieut. Levy?

Ans. the duties properly belong to the Executive Officer, Mr. Lawsinger, the 1st Lieut. W all supposed these duties were put upon Mr. Levy because the Comm. had very great confidence in his skill. I never heard him say so, but we supposed so from this fact.

Question by same. While the U. S. Ship Cyane was at Rio, state whether or not one of her Mid'n was rescued from danger by Lt. Levy? If yea, give all the particulars of the affair and state his conduct throughout the same.

Ans. Whilst at work at the Navy Yard in charge of a gang of armerers some time early in the afternoon, the report reached us that one of the Mid'n named Moores who had charge of one of the gangs, had been assaulted and that Mr. Levy, in rescuing him, had got himself into trouble. I called out to my gang to seize anything they could get hold of and to follow me, and I believe the other officers did the same and we all started off together. We have just got fairly under way when Mr. Levy was seen coming down towards us, waving us back and ordering us to keep the men together under the sheds where they could come at his call. Directly we saw Mr. Levy coming back with Mr. Moores and an American seaman who was the cause of the trouble. This man had been impressed by the Brazilian Press Gang and throwed himself upon the protection of Moores, who refused to give him up to the Admiral, who put his hands on him, Moores, using some approbious expression and Moores knocked him down. When Mr. Levy approached us I saw his hand held in the other rolled up in a handkerchief. I asked him what was the matter. He told us that in warding off a blow aimed at Mr. Moores while down (having been knocked down by the crowd as we heard) he had dislocated his little finger. Mr. Moores thought Mr. Levy saved his life. Mr. Levy told us at the same time that he received a thrust of a bayonet in his side, that bruised him very much as he said. And thereupon the Court adjourned until tomorrow at 10 o'clock A.M.

Tuesday, November 24, A. D. 1854

Court met, pursuant to adjournment. Present: the President, members, Judge Advocate, Mr. Levy, and his counsel. The record of yesterday's proceedings was read by the Judge Advocate and approved. And thereupon the said Levy recalled *Lieut. Peter Turner* who continued as follows.

Question by Mr. Levy. Is Mid'n Moores living or dead?

Ans. I believe he is dead but am not certain; I think I heard of his death some years ago.

Question by same. Look at the paper Marked "Land" [not included] state whether it is in the hand writing of Mid'n Moores or not, as you know or believe.

Ans. I do not know that I ever saw Mr. Moores hand writing. I can't recollect it if I did. I can't say as I ever saw his writing at all.

Question by same. Do you recollect whether Mid'n Moores was arrested soon after the affair testified to by you?

Ans. He was arrested or suspended. I don't recollect which. He was put off duty in consequence of it.

Question by same. State whether or not Don Pedro 1 Emperor of Brazil was in the habit of visiting the Navy Yard at Rio while you were working on the Mast? If yea, what brought him there, as you know or believe?

Ans. He did very often. I think I may way every day and as it appeared to us and as we were told, to hasten the fitting out of a Squadron to go around to St. Catherines to suppress an insurrection.

Question by same. Previous to the affair of Mid'n Moores, did or not, the Emperor notice Lieut. Levy and his party? If so, in what manner? Did he converse with Lieut. Levy? If yes, in what language? Did you understand it?

Ans. The Emperor did take notice of our party and converse with Mr. Levy in French and on the subject of work, I presume, because he pointed to it and appeared to be observing it while talking. I did not understand the language.

Question by same. The next morning after that affair did the Emperor visit the Navy yard? If yea, did you, or not, see him in conversation with Lt. Levy? If so, how near to them were you?

Ans. He did visit the Yard on the next morning and immediately after receiving the salutes of the officers, came up and commenced conversation with Mr. Levy. I was, perhaps, a couple of yards from them.

Question by same. Was Lieut. Levy's hand then in the sling, or not?

Ans. It was.

Question by same. In what language was their conversation? How long did it continue? What was the manner, during it, of the Emperor and of Lt. Levy?

Ans. It was in French. It continued between 15 and 20 minutes I should think. The Emperor's manner was polite, pleasant and Mr. Levy's manner indicated pleasure, satisfaction and gratification.

Question by same. Was there present at that conversation a foreigner who understood French? If so, who was he? How near was he to the Emperor and to you?

Ans. There was a Captain Haddaman our professor of Mathematics and Languages, perhaps I had better say French, as he taught no other language. He had been a Capt in one of the Austrian Emperor's Regiments. He stood within 2 or 3 feet of me, and perhaps a couple of yards from the Emperor.

Question by same. Did or not Capt. Haddaman tell you in English what the Emperor had said to Lt. Levy? If yea, what was it? State also, how soon it was that he gave you this interpretation?

Ans. He did interpret for me the moment the Emperor's back was turned; the substance of the interpretation was that the Emperor complimented Lt. Levy upon the prompt and handsome manner in which he had rushed in and rescued his brother officer and fellow seaman, and wished he had such zealous officers in his own service, and concluded by offering or inviting him to take command of a new Frigate just sent from the U. S., a 60-gun Frigate, taken there by Lt., now Capt., Franklin Buchanan. This was in 1827.

Question by same. Did Capt. Haddaman then state to you what Lt. Levy said to the Emperor in reply to his offer? If so, what was it?

Ans. I do not recollect. I recollect the reply that Mr. Levy made (whether to the Emperor or to the Brazilian Admiral I don't now recollect). The reply expressed gratitude for the honor, but declined its acceptance as he loved his own service so well that he had rather serve in it as a cabin boy than as a Captain in any other service in the world.

Question by same. While the Cyane lay at Rio, was there a boat built for her use? If so, what kind of a boat, who directed the carpenters and superintended her construction and whether or not it was work of difficulty requiring professional knowledge and skill?

Ans. There was a whale boat built, for a gig for the Captain's use. Lt. Levy modeled her, planned her, and superintended the work. It was a work of difficulty and requiring knowledge and skill. Our carpenters knew little about it and were dependent entirely upon Lt. Levy's knowledge in every thing except the labor, even to getting the pieces, picking up one in one place and another in another, from different vessels.

Question by same. Was the boat a staunch and valuable one or not?

Ans. So far as I can recollect she was a very excellent one.

Question by same. Could such a boat have been procured at Rio or not?

Ans. At that time, not, in my opinion. From my knowledge of whale boats, she was a much better one that whale boats usually are.

Question by same. In altering the main mast at Santos, referred to by you yesterday, was it or not a work of greater difficulty than that done at Rio? Was machinery necessary, if so, what, who planned and caused it to be erected and superintended its use?

Ans. After it was out and got on shore, it was a work of more difficulty than that at Rio. I do no recollect as to machinery. In getting it out shears were used, and the fall to the main purchase taken to the Captain. I can't recollect whether the shears were constructed of parts from the ship or rough spars from the shore. Mr. Levy was the ostensible manager of the work. He was on deck, gave the orders and had charge of the work.

Question by same. While the Cyane was at sea, state whether or not the head of the main mast was sprung. If yea, what was thereupon done for the safety of the ship? Who had the active charge of this duty and was it, or not, a duty requiring professional knowledge and skill?

Ans. We discovered it to be sprung while at sea. I do not recollect what was done at this time. I recollect seeing Capt. Elliott and Mr. Levy together on deck. I do not recollect distinctly who had the active charge. It was a duty requiring professional skill.

Question by same. State whether or not Lt. Levy was in the top, attending to this duty, and if so, for how many hours continuously?

Ans. I cannot recollect.

Question by same. What was your age at the period you have referred to and how long had you been in the service?

Ans. I was between 20 and 21. I had been in the service about 6 years and at sea about four and a half.

Testimony was read to witness, pronounced correct and witness dismissed. And thereupon the said Levy called as a witness in his behalf, Lieut. Edmund Lanier, USN, who was duly sworn and testified as follows to wit:

Ans. to 1st general question by Mr. Levy. I am acquainted with Mr. Levy and have known him since 1838.

Ans. to 2nd Do. I served with him about 11 months in the fall of 1839 in the Vandalia. He was Commander of the ship. I served in the capacity of a Master and of an Acting Lieut. I was a passed Mid'n and acting Lt. doing the duty a part of the time of a Master.

Question by Mr. Levy. What was the disposition of the wardroom officers towards Capt. Levy when he took the command of the Vandalia and whether or not his post was thereby rendered a difficult one?

Ans. I do not know what was their disposition.

Question by same. State whether or not he was always zealous in the discharge of his duty as Commander of the ship, and in that respect set a good example to his officers and men?

Ans. He was.

Question by same. What were his personal habits and example in respect to temperance in eating and drinking and in other moral virtues while in this command?

Ans. He was one of the most temperate men I have ever sailed with, both in eating and drinking, a very abstemious man in every respect. He was a perfectly moral man, so far as I was able to judge.

Question by same. Did he or not, take an interest in the instruction and proficiency of the Mid'n and junior officers? If yea, how did he manifest the same?

Ans. He did, by exercising them with the small arms, reefing the topsail, and by exercising them at the great guns.

Question by same. What was the condition of his ship while under his command, in point of order and efficiency, and was he, or not, zealous to secure order and efficiency?

Ans. She was in good order and I considered her very efficient. He was zealous to secure order and efficiency.

Question by same. In what condition was the ship when he took command of her?

Ans. Her discipline was improved on his taking command of her. She was then in ordinary condition.

Question by same. Look on the book now shown to you marked "M" [not included], do you recognize it or not as the Order Book of the Vandalia while under his command?

Ans. I think it is the order book of the Vandalia. I recognize the handwriting of one who was the Yeoman of the ship, in the first of it. I presume it is the same. I may be mistaken as to his being a Yeoman at the time.

Question by same. Look at Book marked "N" [not included]. Is it the book containing the internal regulations of the Vandalia at that time?

Ans. I know that many of the rules and regulations were in force in the ship and I recognize the signature of Mr. Downes, the 1st Lieut. I believe it to be the same.

Question by same. What were his qualifications as a seaman as displayed by him while in command of the Vandalia, in respect to professional knowledge and skill and personal vigilance and acting in the management and navigation of the ship?

Ans. I consider him a thorough seaman. He did exhibit all those qualities while in command of the Vandalia.

Question by the same. Did he or not, often taken upon himself active and difficult duties in the navigation of the ship?

Ans. On one occasion I recollect, while at anchor off Galveston, during the midwatch, the ship was reported to be dragging. He took the deck and got the ship under way in the best possible way, under fore and aft sails. She was dragging rapidly in shore. It would not had answered to have delayed by getting her square sails on her.

Question by same. Do you remember any other instance of his professional activity and efficiency in time of difficulty? If so, state the same.

Ans. I do not recollect any other; but there were several that conveyed to my mind that he was an excellent seaman.

Question by same. State whether or not he manifested zeal in the acquisition of nautical information, not only for the benefit of the ship but for that of the Naval service in general.

Ans. He did. He caused us to sound every half hour or to sound frequently in correcting latitudes and longitudes of Ports on the Coast of Mexico and Texas, which were wrong on Blunts chart of that coast that we were using. He had also, a chart constructed from it.

Question by same. Look at the Chart marked "O" [not included] and state whether or not it is the chart referred to by you; also, whether it correctly sets for the several cruises of the Vandalia, and the soundings made by order of Capt. Levy.

Ans. This is, I think, a copy of the chart that was made aboard the ship. We visited the Ports that these marks indicate. I presume the soundings were correct; there was a great deal of pains taken to get them so. I think Lt. Maffitt projected the chart. I know he jotted down the soundings.

Question by same. In every instance of difficulty and danger which occurred during the cruises of the Vandalia, state whether or not Capt. Levy showed himself cool and collected, active, capable and efficient as a seaman and Commander? On such occasions was he or not, always on deck?

Ans. He did and was.

Question by same. State whether or not by his coolness and skills in the gale at Galveston to which you have referred, the ship was saved from being driven on shore?

Ans. He showed skill by what he did, but she might have been saved if he had not been there.

Question by same. What were his orders and conduct in respect to obeying the signals of the flagship?

Ans. I don't think we ever sailed in a Squadron. He was exceedingly particular that all signals from the flagship should be obeyed immediately.

Question by same. Was or not the Vandalia foremost in obeying my signals or following the motions of the Commodore?

Ans. In a majority of the cases I think she was.

Question by same. State whether or not the service in which he was employed in the Vandalia was a severe and difficult one, and if so, in what respects?

Ans. One portion of the cruise was quite severe. We were cruising off the south coast of Louisiana in June and July, between the South West Pass and the coast of Texas for some 50 or 60 days without being permitted to go in Port, the weather, at that time, being exceedingly warm. The rest of our cruising was such as vessels in the Gulf ordinarily undergo.

Question by same. State whether or not Capt. Levy showed himself attentive to and anxious for the health and comforts of his officers and men? Did he or not, do all in his power to promote their health and comfort?

Ans. I think he did.

Question by same. State whether or not Capt. Levy often exercised his officers and men at general quarters as well as at divisional quarters at great guns and with small arms?

Ans. He did.

Question by same. State whether or not he caused the rules and articles of war for the Navy to be frequently read to the ship's company.

Ans. I believe they were read on the first Sunday of every month, as is usual in men of War.

Question by same. Did he or not during the cruise exhibit the qualities of personal courage and zeal for the honor of his country? Do you remember or not an instance in which these qualities were displayed in an affair with a French officer? If yes, state the same particulars.

Ans. I think he did exhibit those qualities in the course he passed towards the Captain of a French ship, she standing in for our anchorage under the Island of Sacrificest in passing ahead of this French vessel the wind rather headed us off and we carried away some of his head spears. An officer on board of the French vessel ran forward and used some epithets which I understood were of an offensive nature. As soon as we came to anchor Capt. Levy had his boat called away, sent for the 1st Lieut. and told him he must go with him on board of this Frenchman and that he was going on board of her to call the person, if it was the Captain, to account for his language, and if it was the 1st Lieut. of the vessel, he, Mr. Pennington, 1st Lt. of the Vandalia must call him out. He took with him also Mid'n Barboe who spoke French very well. On their return from the Frenchman, I understood, I don't know from which one of those officers, the Frenchman wade a humble apology for his language.

Ans. to 3rd general question by Mr. Levy. I do believe his physically, mentally morally and professionally competent to perform the duties of a Captain in the Navy, and fit for the service.

Question by same. Were you or not promoted, first to the office of Acting Sailing Master, and then of Acting Lieut. by Capt. Levy, and if yea, what led to these promotions?

Ans. I was so promoted. What led to it was, I think, a deficiency in the number of officers on board. My second promotion was in consequency of Lt. Paul having been lost.

Question by the Court. Did you mess with Capt. Levy on board the Vandalia?

Ans. I did not. I think he messed alone.

Question by Judge Advocate. In testifying that the Vandalia was in efficient condition, do you mean to be understood that the state of feeling on board among the officers towards Mr. Levy was such as to promote the efficiency of the service?

Ans. I mean that she was ready for action and would have done good service if called into action. We had some dissatisfied men on board who were inclined to be insubordinate but they were pretty well curbed.

Question by same. Who were the dissatisfied men of whom you speak, who were inclined to be insubordinate?

Ans. Two of them are dead and one of them is furloughed. Lt. Sharp was one, whom Capt. Levy forced to take a pledge of temperance. Lt. Paul was another.

He fell overboard intoxicated, after Capt. Levy had had the deck taken from him for being in that state. Lt. Pennington was the other who has since lost his mind from the use of liquor as it is stated. (The witness stated that he had preferred not to mention the above names.)

Question by Mr. Levy. Though you did not mess with Capt. Levy, state whether or not you have means of knowing as to his habits in eating and drinking, and how did you become acquainted therewith?

Ans. I had such means. I have dined at his table. And thereupon the Court adjourned until tomorrow morning at 10 o'clock, A.M.

Wednesday, November 25, A.D., 1857

Court met pursuant to adjournment. Present: the President, members, Judge Advocate, Mr. Levy and his counsel. The record of yesterday's proceedings was read by the Judge Advocate and approved.

And thereupon the said Lt. Lanier was recalled and continued, as follows, to wit.

Question by Mr. Levy. State whether or not, after the removal of Lt. Pennington and the appointment of Mr. Downes as 1st Lt., the order and discipline of the ship were not much improved?

Ans. The ship appeared to be more harmonious and I thought things appeared to go on better.

Question by same. Was there a boat built on board the Vandalia for the use of the ship? If so, when, what kind of a boat, who superintended the building thereof, and what name was given to her?

Ans. there was a small boat built on board of the ship under the Superintendence of Capt. Levy from some old materials that were on board. The named her the Argus.

Question by same. State whether or not the Mid'n of the Vandalia rowed themselves in this boat, to the school ship Macedonian?

Ans. They were in the habit of using it for that purpose and others.

Question by same. State whether or not Capt. Levy, during his command of the Vandalia, ever attempted, to your knowledge or belief, to molest or interfere with, offend or wound the religious rights or feelings as Christians, of his officers and men. Also, whether or not he always manifested respect for those rights and feelings?

Ans. I have no recollection of his having ever interfered with their rights or feelings in that respect. He did always manifest respect for such rights and feelings, so far as I recollect at this time.

Question by same. Was there a Chaplain on board the Vandalia while under Capt. Levy's command?

Ans. There was not.

Question by same. On Sundays, were not the ship's company mustered, when the weather permitted, and a chapter from the Old Testament and a chapter of the New Testament read, in pursuance of a standing regulation made by Capt. Levy?

Ans. There were.

Question by same. Was the bell tolled for the purpose of calling the ships company to this service, if so, for how long?

Ans. I do not recollect. It is customary to do so, but I do not recollect. All hands were required to attend divine service on board.

Question by same. Did Capt. Levy or not, always personally attend this service?

Ans. He did.

The whole of this witness's testimony was read to him, pronounced correct and the witness dismissed.

And thereupon the said Levy called as a witness in his behalf, Capt. Wm. J. McCluney, USN, who was duly sworn and testified as follows to wit:

Ans. to 1st general question by Mr. Levy. I am acquainted with Mr. Levy and have known him upwards of 40 years.

Ans. to 2nd Do. He has never served with me.

Ans. to 3rd Do. I believe him to be mentally, morally and physically fit for the Navy. I can't speak as to his professional fitness because I have never sailed with him, except from reputation. From that I should say he is fit for it.

Testimony read to witness, pronounced correct and witness dismissed.

And thereupon the said Levy called as a witness in his behalf, Joshua I. Cohen, who was duly sworn and testified as follows, to wit:

Question by Mr. Levy. Where do you reside and what is your occupation?

Ans. I reside in the city of Baltimore. Until very recently I have been a practitioner of Medicine. I have retired.

Question by same. Have you or not, been connected in any way with the Naval service, and if yea, when, how, and for what time?

Ans. I have not been directly connected with the Navy but many years ago was the attending Physician at the naval rendezvous for some weeks, during the absence of the Surgeon stationed there. I think it was in 1826 or 27. It was while Commd. Shubrick commanded these rendezvous.

Question by same. Are you acquainted with Capt. U. P. Levy? If yea, how long have you known him and what has been the nature and degree of your acquaintance, whether professional or social, intimate or otherwise?

Ans. I am acquainted with him; I have known him some 35 or 40 years. I have been intimately acquainted with him socially during this long time.

Question by same. What, during your acquaintance with him, has been his physical condition in respect of health, hardihood, activity, and efficiency, and what is it now?

Ans. He has been always remarkable for a perfect physical condition in respect to health, hardihood, activity and efficiency and the same is his condition now in my opinion.

Question by same. Have you personally observed the moral and mental traits of character of Capt. Levy? If yea, state, according to your knowledge and observation thereof, his moral character and deportment from your first acquaintance with him to the present time? State also, the character of his mind as to strength, quickness and activity.

Ans. I have observed the moral and mental traits of his character. My earliest impressions of him were favorable to him from the circumstance that he was a good son and a good brother, traits of character that were generally known by those who knew him and his family. He was, I believe, the support of his mother, who was a widow, and of his sister, and of his younger brothers. I believe the same characteristics, so far as his *morale* is concerned, attach to him still. His moral character is good. I think his mind is exceedingly quick and active. His deportment, in reference to that point, he has his foibles as most of us have, but I think they are more than outweighed by sterling traits of character. I speak of both character and deportment.

Question by same, being the same as the 3rd general question.

Ans. From what I have known of him I do believe him physically, mentally, professionally and morally competent to perform the duties of a Captain in the Navy, and fit for said service.

Testimony read to witness, pronounced correct, and witness dismissed. And thereupon the said Levy called as a witness in h is behalf, *Lt. John N. Maffitt, USN*, who was duly sworn and testified as follows, to wit:

Ans. to 1st general question by Mr. Levy. I am acquainted with Mr. Levy and have known him since October 1838.

Ans. to 2nd Do. I have served with him, from October 1838 to November, I think, 1839. He was Commander of the Sloop of War Vandalia, one of the vessels of the Gulf Squadron. I was a Passed Mid'n holding the appointment of Acting Lt. and Sailing Master for the greater portion of the time. This was in the Gulf of Mexico.

Question by Mr. Levy. Was the Vandalia, during Capt. Levy's command, the flagship of Commd. Dallas for any time? If so, when and how long?

Ans. She was so when I joined her and remained so until about February 1839, I think, when the Commd. transferred his flag to the Sloop of War Eric, and the Vandalia sailed for the Gulf.

Question by same. What led to your appointment by Capt. Levy as Acting Lt. and Sailing Master? Did the necessity of the service on board said ship require that some one should be promoted to those employments?

Ans. The death of Acting Lt. Paul and the constant indisposition of Lt. Guest, led to my promotion. There was but one officer to keep watch. The ship was without a Sailing Master. Consequently, the necessities of the service did lead to my promotion.

Question by same. State whether or not he was always zealous in the discharge of his duty as commander of the ship and in that respect set a good example to his officers and men?

Ans. He was.

Question by same. What was the condition of his ship while under his command, in point of order and efficiency? And was he or not zealous to secure order and efficiency?

Ans. The ship was efficient in every particular. He was very much so.

Question by same. What were his orders and conduct in respect to obeying the signals of the flagship?

Ans. His orders were very stringent in regard to the officers being exceedingly particular in reference to all matters concerning the duties of the ship and his conduct zealous. The duty referred to included.

Question by same. Was or not the Vandalia foremost in obeying by signals or following the motion of the Commodore?

Ans. She was always very prompt and as a general thing, was foremost.

Question by same. What were his personal habits as known to you, in respect to temperance and other moral virtues?

Ans. He was perfectly temperate, and so far as I could judge from personal observation scrupulously moral.

Question by same. Did he or not take an interest in the instruction and proficiency of the Mid'n and junior officers? If yea, how did he manifest the same?

Ans. He did take in interest in the instruction of the Mid'n. He was particular that the Master should have them on deck at 7 bells at sea to obtain the meridian altitude and I was instructed to furnish them all with chronometer sights and furnish them information upon all points connected with the navigation of the vessel. In moderate weather, at sea, they were frequently exercised in reefing, furling, bending and mending the various topsail. They were also occasionally exercised at one of the guns. They were in the habit of asking permission for the use of a boat, to learn them to pull. I don't recollect any order in relation to the matter.

Question by same. State as to whether he furnished the Midshipmen with quadrants, bow ditch's navigators, and other needful articles to promote their comfort and proficiency?

Ans. The purser of the ship furnished them, I think, by his order.

Question by same. State whether or not the service in which he was employed in the Vandalia was a severe and difficult one, and if so, in what respect?

Ans. The first cruise was in the winter season off Tampico, the Rio Bravo, Vera Cruz and Laguana de Terminos. It was a very boisterous cruise. The second cruise was, for some 3 months, or thereabouts, between Galveston and the South West Pass, during which time we entered no Port.

Question by same. What were his professional qualifications as a seaman, as displayed by him while in command of the Vandalia? Did he, or not, display great knowledge and skill as a seaman?

Ans. He proved himself to be an efficient seaman upon every occasion where his seamanship was called in question.

Question by same. When the ship was in dangerous or difficult positions, did he or not, take personally, an active part in extricating her?

Ans. As Commander of the vessel, he did.

Question by same. Do you remember his conduct on one occasion in a gale at Galveston? If so, state the circumstances.

Ans. I do recollect a circumstance off Galveston where the ship was in considerable danger. We came to anchor about 6 or 7 in the evening, in 6 and a half fathoms of water. At 8 o'clock PM he sent for me, and directed that I should proceed into Galveston Island by day light for the purpose of obtaining observations for the latitude and longitude of the Beacon, or light house. It was incorrectly laid down on the chart. His desire was to have it established correctly, for its application to a chart that I was then projecting by his order. I was consequently excused from watch. Some time after midnight the vessel began to pitch very heavily and my anxiety in regard to her holding on to her anchorage became so great that I went on deck. The weather was threatening and there was heavy ground swell. I found the man in the chains asleep and his line drawing ahead of the vessel. I soon discovered that she was dragging and was at that time in 5 fathoms water. I gave the alarm – all hands were called. The Commander took charge of the deck and while they were heaving up the stern anchor he put the fore and aft sail upon her. When the anchor was up and down he gave her the courses, and sent the men aloft to reef topsails. This conduct on that occasion was prompt and energetic and but for that, there is every probability that she would soon have gone ashore on a 2 and a half fathom bank in close proximity to us.

Question by same. Do you remember any other instance of his professional activity and efficiency in time of difficulty? If so, state the same.

Ans. I do not recollect any other marked instance.

Question by same. In every instance of difficulty and danger which occurred during the cruises of the Vandalia, state whether or not Capt. Levy showed himself cool and collected, active, capable and efficient as a seaman and commander? On such occasion, was he, or not always on deck?

Ans. He was always cool, collected, prompt and efficient in every emergency and always on deck, in such cases.

Question by same. State whether or not he manifested zeal in the acquisition of nautical information, not only for the benefit of the ship but for that of the Naval service in general.

Ans. He did.

Question by same. Look at the lithographed chart, marked "O" [not included], now shown you. Is it a copy of a chart in the preparation of which you took part? If so, does it correctly set forth the soundings and observations made by order of Capt. Levy? State particularly how far the matters contained in it were new.

Ans. This chart (its original) was made by me. It does set forth correctly the soundings and observations made by order of Capt. Levy. The latitude and longitude of Galveston Pt. in the charts then in use was some 35 miles out, as near as I can recollect. The 2-1/2 fathom bank to the eastward northerly of Galveston was not known to exist. The longitude of the Rio Bravo was also erroneous.

Question by same. Are the views of the land contained in it correct? Who took those views?

Ans. They are considered to be very correct. I took some of them. Some were taken by the Mid'n and some by the Commander. The chart has a great deal of matter that was derived from other sources considered to be authentic. I only vouch for that part of the work that belongs exclusively to the Vandalia Commander Levy.

And thereupon the Court adjourned until Friday next at 10 o'clock A.M. (Thursday being yearly observed as a day of Thanksgiving.)

Friday, November 27 A.D. 1857

Court met pursuant to adjournment. Present: the President, members, Judge Advocate, Mr. Levy and his counsel. The record of Wednesday's proceedings was read by the Judge Advocate and approved.

And therefore the said Levy recalled *Lt. J. N. Maffitt* who continued as follows.

Question by Mr. Levy. At the time the chart referred to in your testimony of Wednesday last was published was it or not a valuable contribution to the then existing stock of nautical science and information?

Ans. There was much valuable information in it of considerable importance to the navigator at that period.

Question by same. In what condition was the U. S. ship Vandalia when Commander Levy took command of her? State also, whether or not her strength and efficiency was improved under his command; and if so, in what particulars and by what means?

Ans. He had been in command of the Vandalia some months before I joined her. When I joined the vessel, he hull was not considered to be in every particular in a seaworthy condition. I think she had been on her station over five years, during which time she had never been thoroughly overhauled. I don't recollect any defects in either her spars or riggings, but am under the impression that she was sent North because it was deemed necessary to repair her hull.

Question by same. What was the condition, in respect to efficiency and other useful qualities, of the officers of the wardroom mess at the time you joined the ship?

Ans. I was not a member of the mess when I joined but from by observation, I thought there was both a lack of efficiency and subordination. There were individual exceptions.

Question by same. After Lt. Downes cam on board the Vandalia as 1st Lieut. was there, or not, a marked change for the better, and if so, in what respects?

Ans. There was a marked change for the better, in the personal relations of the officers and consequently of their efficiency.

Question by same. After the advent of Lt. Downer, did Commander Levy interfere with the executive duties of the ship?

Ans. He did not, so far as my memory served me.

Question by same. State whether or not Capt. Levy showed himself attention to and anxious for the health and comfort of his officers and men? Did he or not do all in his power to promote their health and comfort?

Ans. I think he was and did; I don't recollect of any instance to the contrary.

Question by same. State whether or not Capt. Levy during his command of the Vandalia, ever attempted, to your knowledge or belief, to molest or interfere with, offend or wound, the religious rights or feelings as Christians, of his officers and men? Also, whether or not he always manifested respect for those rights and feelings?

Ans. I have no knowledge of any such interference or molestation. He did manifest respect for their rights and feelings in that respect.

Question by same. Was the Christian Sabbath observed on board the Vandalia while under Capt. Levy's command and by his orders? If so, in what manner?

Ans. It was observed on board, and by his orders. The crew was mustered. No mechanical labor was allowed to be performed on that day, and often, a chapter or two from the Bible was read – one from the New and one from the Old Testament. This was a subject of comment among the officers, in regard to the reading a chapter from the New Testament and in connection with the supposed religious faith of the Commander.

Question by same. Did the U. S. Ship Vandalia go to Laguna, Mexico; if so, when, and for what purpose so fare as you know?

Ans. She did go to the anchorage off Laguna, in the month of April, or May (I think April) 1839. I do not recollect the object of her going there.

Question by same. When did the Vandalia sail from Pensacola, and what other U. S. vessels of War were then at that Port?

Ans. She sailed on the 3rd February 1839. I think the Sloop of War Erie was the only other vessel of war then in Port. If there were others there I do not recollect it.

Question by same. When the Vandalia was at Vera Cruz in the spring of 1839, did or not, any U. S. vessels of war arrive at that Port? If yea, give their names and the names of their Commanders.

Ans. The U. S. Sloop of War Ontario, Capt. McKinney arrived while we were there, and the U. S. Packet Brig Consort, Lt. Com'dg, now Capt. Gardiner also came there while we were there.

Question by same. State whether or not Capt. Levy made a visit of exploration up the River Rio Grande del Norte? If so, how, who went with him, how long was he gone, and what, so far as you know, was the object in view?

Ans. I recollect he went up that River as far as Metamoros. I know that Mid'n Marcy accompanied him, and think Purser Brooks did also. They were absent some days from the ship. I do not recollect how many, nor do I recollect the object of said visit.

Question by same. State whether or not Capt. Levy exercised a friendly care over the midshipmen of the Vandalia, in respect to the expenditure of their pay and labored to inculcate on them, prudence and economy.

Ans. He did.

Question by same. Did he or not, during the cruise, exhibit the qualities of personal courage and zeal for the honor of his country? Do you remember, or not, an instance in which these qualities were displayed in an affair with a French officer? If yea, state the same.

Ans. He did. I recollect well the circumstance to which the question refers. In entering the harbor of Sacrificios in passing a French Sloop of War, we carried away her flying jib boom and with that, the fore royal mast. The 1st Lieut. of the Vandalia was sent on board to make an apology, which was not courteously received. At the time of the accident, the Commander of the French Sloop of War, from the forecastle of his ship, made use of the most insulting and provoking language, most of which was personal to the Commander of the Vandalia. Upon my taking charge of the deck after the anchorage of the vessel I reported to Commd. Levy the language and the manner of the French Captain. My report was corroborated by Surgeon Smith and Mid'n Barbot and Wait. These gentlemen were conversant with the French language. When Commd. Levy became convinced that the Frenchman had been officially as well as personally insulting to him, he ordered his boat to be manned and directed that Mid'n Barbot and Wiat, in consequence of their understanding French, should accompany him on board of the French vessel. He was absent about half an hour. On his return, he ordered the Mid'n who had accompanied him to inform me, as officer of the deck, of the result of his demand of the French Captain for an apology, both official and personal. They informed me officially that the French Commander, upon Capt. Levy's peremptory demand for a prompt and unequivocal apology made it upon his quarterdeck.

Question by same. Who was the officer of the deck when the accident to the French ship occurred?

Ans. Lieut. Pennington, the 1st Lieut. of the vessel. It was "all hands" at the time.

Question by same. Was, or not, Capt. Levy below at the time of the accident?

Ans. I think not. All hands had been called to bring ship to anchor, and to the best of my knowledge and belief, he was on deck.

Cross Examined by Judge Advocate. In speaking of Mr. Levy's conduct during the time he commanded the Vandalia, do you mean that his conduct and deportment were always such, as should, in your judgment, should characterize a Commander in the Navy?

Ans. On all occasions except one, I did not consider it.

Question the same. Was his ordinary deportment or manner, in your judgment, free from objection in one exercising Command in the Navy?

Ans. His manner was peculiar. I can't say that it was objectionable. It might be so to those who were hunting up objections.

Question by same. Was his ordinary deportment when in the performance of duty such as you would approve?

Ans. It was.

Question by same. Was it always so, except on the one occasion you before mentioned?

Ans. Sometimes I did not think it was so but the occasions were rare and generally from misconception. When I first knew him, his manner, while on duty, struck me unpleasantly. That wore off as I knew him better.

Question by same. In what respect was his manner peculiar?

Ans. I can not answer – save in regard to peculiarities of voice and manner.

Question by same. Was his language peculiar, and if so, in what respect?

Ans. It was not.

Question by same. What was the one occasion you mentioned? I do not ask for the details but a statement of the occasion.

Ans. It was the indecorous punishment of boy on board the vessel, ordered and superintended by himself.

Question by same. In the performance or ordinary duty, did he, in your judgment, exhibit familiarity with the duties pertaining to his rank?

Part III: Witnesses on behalf of Uriah Phillips Levy

Ans. He did.

Question by same. Was not his treatment of his officers frequently harsh and his manner to them unkind?

Ans. I can't say that it was; although I have known him to be very harsh, on occasions when there was presumed neglect of duty.

Question by same. Do you recollect no occasion of an exposure of officers and men, or either, to a needless danger?

Ans. I do not recollect.

Question by same. Did he, or not introduce unusual punishments on any other occasions than the one to which you have referred?

Ans. He did, that were then unusual.

Question by same. What were they?

Ans. They were numerous, or various.

Question by same. Was there anything unusual in the arrangements ordered by him in respect to any of the appointments of the vessel? And if so, what?

Ans. There were no such unusual arrangements that I recollect. The guns were fitted as is usual. The only peculiarity I recollect about them was in their color, which was blue.

Direct examination resumed.

Question by Mr. Levy. Did not Capt. Levy while in command of the Vandalia, endeavor, as far as practicable, to dispense with punishment by the lash? Were not the various punishments to which you have referred intended by him, as you believe, as substitutes for the use of the lash?

Ans. Such was the case, although the lash was not abolished.

Question by same. Was not the amount of flogging on board the Vandalia, during the time you were in her, less in proportion to the time, and number of her crew, than in other vessels in which you served about that time?

Ans. I never made a comparison, and could not, therefore, answer directly to the question.

Question by the same. Did not the fact of the small number of lashes inflicted on board the Vandalia while under Capt. Levy's command, attract notice on her final return to the U. S. and was it not commented on the public press?

Ans. I did not return in the Vandalia and therefore, do not know as to the comments of the press.

Question by same. State whether or not Capt. Levy, while in command of the Vandalia, invented and brought into successful use a contrivance for preventing the waver being blown off the priming, when about to discharge the great guns in windy weather? If yea, state what it was.

Ans. I do not recollect it.

Testimony read to witness, pronounced correct and witness dismissed. And thereupon the said Levy called as a witness in his behalf, *Dr. Wm. Jones* who was duly sworn and testified as follows, to wit:

Question by Mr. Levy. Have you been connected with the Navy, or the Army? If so, in what capacity, and for what time and where do you reside?

Ans. I have not been connected with the Navy. I have been connected with the army in the War of 1812, attached to the medical Staff, from 1813, to some time in 1815. I now reside in Washington City, practicing medicine, from 1829 to 1839, and from 1841 to 1845, I was Post Master of this city.

Question by same. Are you acquainted with Capt. U. P. Levy? If yea, how long have you known him, and what has been the nature and degree of your acquaintance, whether professional or social, intimate or otherwise?

Ans. I am acquainted with him, have known him upwards of 30 years, have had a good deal of social intercourse with him. Our acquaintance has been quite intimate, more so at an early period than at a later one.

Question by same. Have you personally observed the moral and mental traits of character of Capt. Levy? If yea, state according to your knowledge and observation thereof, his moral character and deportment from your first acquaintance with him to the present time. State also, the character of his mind, as to strength, quickness and activity.

Ans. I have had many opportunities of observing them. His moral character and deportment have always been good. I have regarded him as an honorable and correct gentleman in all the relations of life that I have had an opportunity of observing. I should say the character of his mind is very good, excellent.

Question by same, being same as 3rd general question.

Ans. I should be unwilling to express any opinion as to his fitness for the service professionally. I think he is morally, mentally and physically fit for the office he is aspiring to.

Testimony read, pronounced correct and witness dismissed. And thereupon the said Levy called as a witness in his behalf, Capt. Wm. L. Hudson, USN, who was duly sworn and testified as follows, to wit:

Ans. to 1st general question by Mr. Levy. I am acquainted with U. P. Levy and have known him for 30 years or more.

Ans. to 2nd Do. We have never served together.

Ans. to 3rd Do. I have never sailed with him and do not speak of his professional fitness. I do consider him mentally, morally and physically fit for the service.

Testimony read to witness, pronounced correct and witness dismissed, whereupon the Court adjourned until tomorrow morning at 10 A.M.

Saturday, November 28, A.D. 1857

Court met pursuant to adjournment. Present: the President, members, judge Advocate, Mr. Levy and his counsel. The record of yesterday's proceedings was read by the Judge Advocate and approved. And thereupon the said Levy called as a witness in his behalf, *R. M. Price, Esq.*, who was duly sworn and testified as follows, to wit:

Question by Mr. Levy. What is your occupation and place of residence?

Ans. I reside in Trenton, New Jersey. I have no professional occupation at present, was Governor of the State of New Jersey, my official term of three years, expired in January last. I was a Member of the 32nd Congress and was 12 years in the Navy as a Purser, from 1840 to 1851.

Question by Mr. Levy. Are you acquainted with Capt. U. P. Levy? If yea, how long have you known him and what has been the nature and degree of your acquaintance, whether professional or social intimate or otherwise?

Ans. I am acquainted with him and have known him for the last 12 to 15 years. I have frequently met him socially. Our acquaintance has been intimate, our relations extremely kind and agreeable.

Question by same. Have you personally observed the moral and mental traits of character of Capt. Levy? If yea, state according to your knowledge and observation, thereof, his moral character and deportment from your first acquaintance with him to the present time. State also, the character of his mind as to strength quickness and activity.

Ans. I have observed him in those respects no farther than I generally observe those with whom I associate. I have always considered his moral character and deportment good and his position very high in social life. I have always considered him a gentleman of great intelligence, possessing a sensitive quick and chivalrous mind, and a gentleman of decided ability, of unusual strength of mind, I should say – unusual.

Ans. to 3rd general question. I should consider him eminently fit under all the heads mentioned in the question, except professionally; having never served with him and I am probably not competent to form an opinion of him in that respect.

Ans. to 4th general question. I never have observed in him any such temper or disposition as was calculated to impair his efficiency or mar the harmony of the service. Knowing that great prejudice existed against him amongst officers of the Navy, I scrutinized him more closely that I otherwise would have done; and have never observed anything objectionable at all in him as a gentleman, nor was any fact ever stated to me that has caused any change in my appreciation and estimate of his character.

Testimony read to witness, pronounced correct and witness dismissed. And thereupon the said Levy called as a witness in his behalf, *Peter G. Washington, Esq.*, who was duly sworn and testified as follows, to wit:

Question by Mr. Levy. Where do you reside? What is and has been your occupation?

Ans. I reside in Washington. I was Asst. Sect'y of the Treasury under the last administration.

Question by same. Are you acquainted with Capt. U. P. Levy? If yea, how long have you known him and what had been the nature and degree of your acquaintance, whether professional or social, intimate or otherwise?

Ans. I first heard of him in a manner to impress the fact upon my memory, as early as 1817 or 1818. I have been personally acquainted with him for, perhaps, 20 years and for the last few years, intimately. Our acquaintance has been of a social character.

Question by same. Have you personally observed the moral and mental traits of character of Capt. Levy, if yea, state according to your knowledge and observation thereof, his moral character and deportment, from your first acquaintance with him to the present time? State also, the character of his mind as to strength, quickness and activity.

Ans. My acquaintance and intimacy with him during the last few years have afforded me opportunities to become acquainted with his character and have enabled me to form opinions upon those subjects. I consider both his moral character and deportment unexceptionable. He is strictly temperate in his habits, and circumspect and correct in his deportment. In my opinion, he has an uncommonly strong, quick and active mind.

Ans. to 3rd general question. So far as I am capable of forming a judgment of the qualifications for a profession to which I do not belong, my opportunities of judging having been aided by frequent conversations with him upon professional subjects and incidents, I consider him eminently qualified in all four particulars specified in the question.

Ans. to 4th Do. I never have observed in him any such temper, or disposition as was calculated to impair his efficiency, or mar the harmony of the service. I should, perhaps, add, that he possesses the necessary temper and tone of authority for the position of a Commander in the Navy, but the exercise thereof ought not necessarily to mar the harmony of the service.

Question by same. While in the Treasury Dept had you, and if any, what official connection with the Revenue Cutter service? If yea, did this give you opportunity to become acquainted with the qualifications required in a Commander in the Navy?

Ans. In my prior service in the Treasury Dept as a clerk, from 1822 to 1829, I had a good deal to do with the Revenue Cutters and remember to have had occasion to prepare instructions for building two cutters in Baltimore. I think their names were "Pulaski" and "Marion." When I entered the Treasury in 1853, as Asst. Sect'y, I gave quite as much attention, if not more, to that branch of the public service than others which fell under my supervision. I prepared a report to the President recommending material modifications of the Revenue Service, which were adopted by him, in part, then, and the residue at a subsequent period. At a subsequent period I prepared a new set of regulations for the management of the Cutters, and the government of their officers, which, I believe is still in force. It was a part of my effort, whilst in the Treasury to improve the character and efficiency of that branch of the service; amongst other things, by superseding the employment of officers who had not been bred to the sea, and appointing those only who had. In the course of the examinations, inquiries and conversations which I held with nautical men and others, with a view to these reforms, I suppose I acquired a conception very unusual to a landsman of the qualifications required, both for good seamanship and for efficient command.

Testimony read to witness, pronounced correct and witness dismissed. And thereupon the said Levy called as a witness in his behalf, *Capt. L. M. Powell, USN*, who was duly sworn and testified as follows, to wit:

Ans to 1st general question. In 1817, on board the Franklin he was a Lieut., I was an Acting Mid'n. We served together in that vessel from March 1817 to the spring of 1818. He was also a passenger on board the North Carolina in 1825, I think, in which vessel I was a Mid'n, a passenger from the U. S. to join the Mediterranean Squadron. I have had no other service with him.

Question by same. Have you personally observed the moral and mental traits of character of Capt. Levy? If yea, state according to your knowledge and observation thereof, his moral character and deportment from your first acquaintance with him to the present time. State also, the character of his mind as to strength, quickness and activity.

Ans. I have observed his moral and mental traits of character as much as a man observes those traits amongst his acquaintance. His moral character is excellent, unimpeachable, so far as my observation has gone, or by knowledge. I know nothing impairing either the strength, quickness or activity of his mind, in my opinion.

Question by same. How did he perform his professional duties while you served together, efficiently or otherwise?

Ans. I was too young to judge in 1817 and 18 and in 1825 he was not on duty. I know nothing against his having performed his duty properly at any time.

Ans. to 3rd general question. I know nothing of Mr. Levy, further than I have stated. I have had no opportunity to form an opinion of him in this respect of any value. I know nothing to impair his physical, mental or moral qualifications; nothing that would impair them in my judgment. My opportunities would enable me to form a very good opinion of the general correctness of his deportment in social life, as I have met him frequently nearly every year within the last 40 years when we were in this country together.

Ans. to 4th Do. I never did discover in him any such temper or disposition as was calculated to impair his efficiency or mar the harmony of the service. On the contrary, he has appeared to me to be a humane and obliging man in all his private relations in life.

Testimony read to witness, pronounced correct, and witness dismissed. And thereupon the said Levy called as a witness in his behalf, *David S. Coddington*, who was duly sworn and testified as follows, to wit:

Question by Mr. Levy. Where do you reside? State the former official position in the City of New York of your father, the late Jonathan I. Coddington.

Ans. I reside in the City of New York. He (my father) has been Governor of the Alms House, a member of the legislature and Post Master of New York City from 1835 to 1842.

Question by same. Do you know Capt. U. P. Levy? If yea, how long have you known him and what has been the nature and degree of your acquaintance with him? Did it, or not, begin in your father's family and state whether or not he was on intimate social terms with the family?

Ans. I have known him since 1841. He has been on intimate terms with the family since 1841, up to the present time; seen each other almost daily when he was in New York.

Question by same (being same as the 3rd general question). So far as I am capable of judging, I do, certainly believe him mentally, morally, physically and professionally competent to perform the duties of a Captain in the Navy and fit for said service.

Ans. to 4th Do. I do not recollect a single instance in which his conduct was not governed by good sense and strict integrity.

Question by same. Had you or not, at any time, at the request of Capt. Levy, a conversation with the Hon. John Y. Mason, late Sect'y of the Navy of the U. S. as to the application of Capt. Levy to said Sect'y, to be employed in active duty as a Captain? If yea, state fully what Mr. Mason said to you on the subject?

[In explanation of the above question, the Counsel for Mr. Levy stated that he proposes hereafter to put in evidence the written application referred to in the question, and also stated that Mr. Mason is absent from the country and not within reach of the Court's process.]

The Judge Advocate *objected* to the question, that there is nothing in the explanation by the Counsel to take the question out of the rule which excludes mere "hearsay." Thereupon the Court was cleared, and upon consideration is of opinion that the question is improper.

Thereupon the Court was re-opened and its decision announced by the Judge Advocate.

The testimony of the last witness was thereupon read to him, pronounced correct and witness dismissed. And thereupon the said Levy called as a witness in his behalf *Dr. John B. Blake*, who was duly sworn and testified as follows, to wit:

Question by Mr. Levy. Where do you reside, and what is your occupation? State whether or not you are acquainted with Capt. U. P. Levy, and if year, how long? State whether such acquaintance began in the family of your father, the late James H. Blake?

Ans. I live in this city and at present hold the office of Commissioner of Public Buildings. I know Capt. Levy well. I have been acquainted with him, I think, about 40 years. Such acquaintance did begin in the family of my father, at one time Mayor of this city for a number of years.

Question by same. Have you personally observed the moral and mental traits of character of Capt Levy? If yea, state, according to your knowledge and observation thereof, his moral character and deportment from your first acquaintance with him to the present time? State also, the character of his mind as to strength, quickness and activity.

I have been very intimate with him and have had ample opportunities to observe his character and conduct, both his mental and moral character. I have never observed anything in his conduct that was not perfectly consistent with a high-toned gentleman. He has always appeared to me to be a very sensible, intelligent gentleman, a man of quick perception and good judgment.

Ans. to 3rd general question. I should think from my acquaintance with him that he is mentally, morally and physically fit to perform any duties belonging to his profession. I am not an officer of the Navy and therefore can't speak of his professional qualifications.

Ans. to 4th Do. I never have discovered any such temper or disposition in him as was calculated to impair his efficiency, in my judgment. He was always amicable and polite.

Testimony read to witness, pronounced correct and witness dismissed; whereupon the Court adjourned until 10 o'clock A.M. of Monday next.

Monday, November 30, A. D., 1857

Court met pursuant to adjournment. Present: the President, members, Judge advocate, Mr. Levy and his counsel. The record of Saturday's proceedings was read by the Judge advocate and approved. And thereupon the said Levy called as a witness in his behalf, *Richard S. Coxe, Esq.*, who was duly sworn and testified as follows, to wit:

Question by Mr. Levy. Where do you reside, and what is your occupation?

Ans. I reside in the City of Washington. My occupation is that of a lawyer.

Question by same. Have you, or not, had any connection with the Navy of the US; if so, what was it and when?

Ans. the only connection I have had with the Navy was acting as Judge Advocate during the administration of President Adams (John Q.) and a part of the prior one of President Monroe.

Question by same. Are you acquainted with Capt. U. P. Levy? If yea, for how long? State also, the origin, nature and degree of your acquaintance with him.

Ans. My impression is that during the time I acted as Judge Advocate I acted as such in two cases in which Mr. Levy was the accused. One I distinctly recollect, which occurred in 1827, I think. My acquaintance with him originated in that. I have had no great acquaintance with him from that time to the present day. I have met him occasionally since.

Ans. to 3rd general question. In answer to this question I can hardly speak as an expert. All I can say is I have no recollection of ever having heard anything to his disparagement in relation to his moral character, his professional character, or his physical ability. So far as I can judge from the sources I have mentioned, I should say that I do consider him morally, mentally, physically and professionally competent to perform the duties of a Capt in the Navy and fit for such service.

Testimony read to witness, pronounced correct and witness dismissed. And thereupon the said Levy called as a witness in his behalf *John James Abert, Esq.*, who was duly sworn and testified as follows, to wit:

Question by Mr. Levy. Where do you reside and what is your former and present official employment?

Ans. I reside in this city. I have been a Col. in the Army since 1838 and am now Chief of the Corps of Topographical Engineers, and have been such for many years.

Ans. to 1st general question. I think I have known Mr. Levy nearly, or about 40 years. Our acquaintance has been reasonably familiar, always very friendly when we meet, altogether of a social character.

Ans. to the 3rd Do. Of his professional fitness I can say nothing. The other points of the question I answer affirmatively. I always considered him a gentleman and a man of intelligence.

Testimony read to witness, pronounced correct and witness dismissed. And thereupon the said Levy called as a witness in his behalf, *Purser Levi D. Slamon USN,* who was duly sworn and testified as follows, to wit:

Question by Mr. Levy. Are you or not, connected with the Naval service? If yea, in what capacity and how long?

Ans. I am a Purser in the U. S. Navy and have been in the service 11 years.

Question by same. Do you know Capt. U. P. Levy; if yea, how long have you known him and what has been the nature and degree of your acquaintance with him, whether professional or social, intimate or otherwise?

Ans. I have known him some 13 years. I have never had any professional connection with him. Our acquaintance has been entirely social. I have had frequent discussions with him upon professional topics.

Ans. to 3rd general question. I think him in all the particulars specified in the question eminently fit for the service.

Question by Mr. Levy. State whether or not you were at any time editor of a daily newspaper in the City of New York, if yea, when and what was the name of the paper?

Ans. From 1836 to 1845 I was connected with the press in New York City. During that time I edited three papers, the *New Era,* the *Plebian* and the *New York Globe,* successively.

Question by same. State whether or not Capt. Levy, at various times, furnished to you for publication in the papers edited by you, various articles relating to the interests of the Naval service? If yea, were they published in your paper?

Ans. I have a distinct recollection of publishing a number of articles furnished by Capt. Levy and Major Noah (I can't distinguish them now) upon subjects connected with the Navy, from Capt. Levy, particularly, upon the subject of the abolition of corporeal punishment by the lash, in the Navy. It was from those articles that I judged of his fitness for the service.

Testimony read to witness, pronounced correct and witness dismissed. And thereupon the said Levy called as a witness in his behalf *John Etheridge, Esq.*, who was duly sworn and testified as follows, to wit:

Question by Mr. Levy. State your part and present connection with the Naval service and the Navy Department.

Ans. I reside in Washington. In 1818 I joined Commd. Hull at Charleston Navy Yard as his Clerk and remained with him as such until 1823, when he gave up that charge. I re-joined him at Norfolk in 1823 when he was ordered to the command of the Pacific Squadron and remained with him in that capacity and a portion of the time as acting Chaplain, and performing duties as Storekeeper and Purser on that station, until the return of the Ship to New York in, I think, 1827. I again joined him in 1829, when ordered to the Command of the Washington Navy Yard. My services then were in connection with the duties of Navy Agent imposed by law upon the Commandant of that Navy Yard, in the performance of which I continued until the duties of Navy Agent were separated and confided to a citizen. I was then appointed Clerk to the Commandant of the Yard and continued with him (Commd. Hull) until he retired from that commission in 1835. I, however, remained at the Yard in the same capacity until the latter part of 1838, under different officers. In that year I again joined Commd. Hull as his Secretary to the Mediterranean Squadron, and performed in that cruise with him returning in 1841 when I was called to an office in Washington under the Treasury Dept, being in the 4th Auditors Office, until 1849 when I was invited to accept the Chief Clerkship of the Navy Dept, in which office I continued until the year 1853, when I resigned, and afterwards accepted, at the special request of the then Sect'y of the Navy, Mr. Dobbin, of the office of the principal corresponding Clerk of the Navy Dept which office I now hold. This narration has been given from memory, subject to all the allowances to be made for the period of time it embraces.

Question by Mr. Levy. Are you acquainted with Capt. U. P. Levy? If yea, how long have you known him and what has been the nature and degree of your acquaintance, whether professional or social, intimate or otherwise?

Ans. I am acquainted with him and have known him personally since 1832. Our acquaintance has not been professional. It has been friendly and free.

Ans. to 3rd general question. I do believe him mentally, morally, physically and professionally competent to perform the duties of a captain in the Navy and fit for said service. I know of no disqualification.

Ans. to 4th Do. I have not discovered any such temper or disposition in him as was calculated to impair his efficiency or mar the harmony of the service. On the contrary, I have looked upon him as a man of magnanimous sentiment, peacefully inclined but prompt to resent indignities.

Testimony read to witness, pronounced correct and witness dismissed. And thereupon the said Levy called as a witness in his behalf *Benj O. Taylor, Esq.*, who was duly sworn and testified as follows, to wit:

Question by Mr. Levy. What is your residence and occupation?

Ans. I reside in Washington. Have no special employment at present.

Question by same. Are you or not acquainted with Capt. U. P. Levy? If yea, for how long? When and where did you acquaintance begin and in what capacity were you at the time?

Ans. I am acquainted with him. My acquaintance with him began I think in December 1817, on board the Franklin, the Flag Ship of Commd. Stewart. I was then attached to the American Legation on its way to England. Richard Rush was then the Minister to England.

Question by same. What was Mr. Levy's deportment as an officer and a gentleman during the voyage of the Franklin to England, so far as the same fell under your observation?

Ans. I can not speak of his deportment as an officer. As a gentleman, it was unexceptionable, so far as I know.

Question by same. State whether or not your acquaintance with him has continued since 1817 and what has been its nature and degree?

Ans. It has. I have been in the habit of meeting him off and on every 2 or 3 years from that time to the present. In his visits to Washington he has generally visited me and our acquaintance has been kept up in that way.

Ans. to 3rd general question. I have no right to believe to the contrary of his fitness for the navy in the several respects mentioned in the question. I have never seen any improprieties in his conduct in my life.

Ans. to 4th Do. I have never discovered any such temper or disposition in him as was calculated to impair his efficiency or mar the harmony of the service.

Testimony read to witness, pronounced correct and witness dismissed. And thereupon the said Levy called as a witness in his behalf, *George S. Watkins, Esq.*, who was duly sworn and testified as follows, to wit:

Question by Mr. Levy. What is your residence and occupation?

Ans. I reside in Georgetown; am a Clerk in the Navy Dept, Assistant Corresponding Clerk.

Question by same. Were you are not employed in the Navy Dept in the year 1844? If yea, in what capacity and what was then your special duty?

Ans. I was, and had charge of the records of Courts Martial.

Question by same. State whether or not, in the winter or spring of 1844, the records of Courts Martial and other documents in the archives of the Navy Dept, relating to U. P. Levy, in the several offices held by him in the Navy, from that of Sailing Master to that of Commander, both inclusive, were laid before the Naval Committee of the Senate, in reference to his nomination as Capt. If so, for how long a time were said documents in possession of said committee?

[To the foregoing question the Judge Advocate *objected* that the enquiry propounded in the question is entirely irrelevant to the enquiry involved in this investigation.]

Thereupon the Court was cleared and upon consideration, is of opinion that the question may be answered, reserving the point as to the *effect* to be given to it for future consideration.

Thereupon the Court was re-opened and its decision announced by the Judge Advocate.

Ans. At the time mentioned they were gathers together and taken from my possession for the purpose, as I understood at the time, of being sent to the Senate. I presume they were sent. They remained out of my possession a considerable time. I can't say how long; I presumed they were taken with reference to his nomination for promotion. There was no other reason for taking them that I was aware of.

Testimony read to witness, pronounced correct and witness dismissed, whereupon the Court adjourned until tomorrow morning at 10 o'clock A.M.

Thursday, December 1st A.D. 1857

Court met pursuant to adjournment. Present: the President, members, Judge Advocate, Mr. Levy and his counsel. The record of yesterday's proceedings was read by the Judge Advocate and approved. And thereupon the said Levy called as a witness in his behalf, *Geo. F. DeLaRoche*, who was duly sworn and testified as follows, to wit:

Question by Mr. Levy. Where do you reside and what is your occupation?

Ans. I reside in Georgetown. I am a Civil Engineer and Architect; at present, I am draftsman of the Bureau of Yards and Docks.

Question by same. State whether or not you were ever connected with the Merchant Marine Service? If yea, when, in what capacity and how long?

Ans. I was, from 1804 until 1812, first apprenticed to Lloyd Jones, the brother of Wm. Jones who was afterwards Sect'y of the Navy and passed through the several grades to that of a Captain in the Merchant service.

Question by same. When did you first become connected with the Naval service of the U. S. and what has been your service therein?

Ans. In April or May 1812, as volunteer Master's Mate, I was first ordered to the N. Y. station, where I remained until September 1812, thence to the Constellation Frigate, then fitting out here, of which I remained 1st Masters Mate until the summer of 1813, then I took charge of a Gun Boat until September 1813 when I joined the Eric Sloop of War as Sailing Master, when I remained until Capt. Ridgley was ordered to Lake Ontario, when I took command of the Eric. I remained in her until the spring of 1815 when I got a furlough and took command of a Merchant Ship. In 1819 I resumed active duty in the Navy as Sailing Master of the Constellation again the same year I joined the John Adams in the same capacity. In June 1825 I resigned.

Question by same. Are you or not, acquainted with Capt. U. P. Levy? If yea, when, where and under what circumstances did you first become acquainted with him? Was he or not then an apprentice to John Coulter of Philadelphia? How long had he then been such apprentice?

Ans. We were boys together nearly of same age, he apprenticed to James or John Coulter, I don't recollect which, and I to Lloyd Jones. This was our first acquaintance. It was at Philadelphia. This was about 1806, or 1807; I can't say how long he had been apprenticed then. We met as boys attached to ships near each other. During the embargo we went to a school kept by an old English gentleman named Talbot Hamilton, who had been a Lt. in the British Navy.
Mr. Levy, Commd. Charles W. Skinner and myself were in the same class, studying navigation.

Question by same. Was Mr. Hamilton a qualified teacher and what was the character of his school?

Ans. It was then thought the best school in Philadelphia for navigation. It was on the account I was sent there.

Question by same. Did, or not, Mr. Hamilton take special interest in the proficiency of his pupils? If yea, how did he show such special interest?

Ans. He certainly was a good teacher. I think he did take special interest in the proficiency of his pupils and exhibited by his attention to them. He used to take his pupils in to see his picture gallery when he was pleased with them.

Question by same. State whether or not Capt. Levy had been to sea and if yea, how long, in what vessels and what capacity, as you know or believe, before joining the Naval School of Mr. Hamilton?

Ans. I am unable to say what vessels. He had been to sea; Mr. Coulter owned a ship, the Rittenhouse and, I think, 3 brigs. I can't say how long he had been to sea then. It was in the capacity of a boy, before the Mast.

Question by same. How long did you and Capt. Levy attend the Naval School to which you have referred and when he left the school did he go to sea, and if so, in what vessel and who was her Commander?

Ans. We attended during the embargo, 6 or 8 months at least. Can't say positively as to the time. I went to sea myself as soon as the embargo was over.
I am unable to say whether he did so or not.

Question by same. Who was the commander of Mr. Coulter's Ship, the Rittenhouse, and what was his character as a seaman and commander? What became of her?

Ans. Capt. Maffitt. I have always heard him spoken of as a first rate Commander; I don't recollect what became of her.

Question by same. State whether or not Mr. Coulter owned a Brig called the Polly and Betsy, Capt. Silsbee? If yea, was Capt. Levy, at any time, and when, Mate of said Brig?

Ans. I have a recollection of the name and I know Capt. Levy was a Mate on board one of his Brigs; but I can not say it was that one.

Ans. to 2nd general question. We have never served together at sea, but served on the same station, the N. Y. Station, in 1812; can't say how long. He was a Sailing Master attached to the yard or to one of the vessels. I can't say which. I recollect the Ship Alert was there.

Ans. to 3rd Do. I am scarcely fit to speak of his fitness for a Captain, as I have never reached that rank. He certainly was a seaman. I have never known any thing against his moral character.

Testimony read to witness, pronounced correct and witness dismissed. And thereupon the said Levy called as a witness in his behalf *Capt. Wm. D. Salter, USN,* who was duly sworn and testified as follows, to wit:

Ans. to 1st general question. I am acquainted with Mr. Levy and have known him, I think, at least 25 years; I think 30 years.

Ans. to 2nd Do. We have not served together in the same ship. We were in the same Squadron together, on the Coast of Brazil under Commd. Elliott; He as 1st Lieut. of the Cyane; I as 1st Lieut. of the Macedonia Frigate, under command of Commd. Biddle. I think this was in 1826 and a part of 1827. I can't say how long.

Question by same. While you were together in the Squadron in what manner did he perform the duties of Executive Officer of the Cyane, as you know or believe? Were you on board that ship, if yea, how often, what was her condition as to discipline and efficiency so far as the same depended on him?

Ans. The ship was kept in very fine order. I was on board of her several times, I can't say how often. Her condition as to discipline and efficiency was very good, so far as I knew. If there had been any deficiency Commd. Eliott would have discovered and reported it to Commd. Biddle; there is no doubt about that. I recollect on one occasion his beating out of the harbor at Rio in very pretty style, which was a rare thing at that time.

Ans to 3rd general question. So far as my knowledge of him extends, he is competent to perform the duties of a Captain in the Navy and fit for such service.

Ans to 4th Do. I never discovered any such temper or disposition in him as to impair his efficiency or mar the harmony of the service.

Testimony read to witness, pronounced correct and witness dismissed. And thereupon the said Levy called as a witness in his behalf *Commd. James Glynn,USN,* who was duly sworn and testified as follows, to wit:

Question by Mr. Levy. Were you acquainted with Mid'n John W. Moores, now deceased? If yea, state whether or not you had knowledge of his understanding.

Ans. I was acquainted with him and corresponded with him. I think I would know his writing.

Question by same. Look on the paper now shown to you, mark and state whether or not you believe the same to be in the proper handwriting of said Moores.

Ans. I believe it is.

Testimony read to witness, pronounced correct and witness dismissed. And thereupon the said Levy called as a witness in his behalf *Asakel S. Levy, Esq.*, who was duly sworn and testified as follows, to wit:

Question by Mr. Levy. What is your residence and occupation?

Ans. I reside in the city of New York and am a lawyer.

Question by same. Are you, or not, a relation of Capt. U. P. Levy? Have you, or not, lived in his family; if yea, during what period and what has been and is the degree of your familiarity with his affairs?

Ans. I am his nephew. I have lived in his family, was brought up and educated by him. I am and have been his attorney at law and in fact, am familiar with his affairs.

Question by same. State whether or not you have any knowledge of the preparation and publication, by Capt. Levy at any time prior to the year 1855, of articles in relation to the interests of the Naval service? If yea, state generally their subject, the time when prepared and published, and how published?

Ans. I have such knowledge. The subjects were various. The most prominent that I can recollect was upon the subject of Naval construction, Naval discipline and the abolition of corporeal punishment in the Navy – I remember some as early as 1845 and continued every year from that time to 1855. They were published in the papers of the City of New York. The Courier and Engineer and others also in Virginia papers and I think in papers of this City.

Question by same. Look on the chart Marked "O" [not included] and state whether or not the same was lithographed and published by Capt. Levy at his own and what expense, and what you know as to its circulation?

Ans. It was lithographed and published at his expense – I don't know precisely at what expense, but I think between $300 and $400, I paid some of the bills myself. Notices were inserted in the leading journals of the City of New York that copies of it could be had "gratis" by applying at my office in Wall Street. These notices were published in other cities. I had a great number of personal and written applications for them and gave them in pursuance thereof.

Question by same. Look on the Manual of Rules for Men of War, Marked "P" [not included] and state at whose expense it was published and what you know of its circulation.

Ans. It was published by Capt. U. P. Levy and at his own expense and distributed by him gratuitously, through the house of Appleton and Co., Broadway, New York. I do not recollect the time. It was written the last 2 or 3 years.

Question by same. State whether or not Capt. Levy published, at his own, and what expense, and if yea, when, a lecture on the Navy, delivered in 1852 by the Hon. F. P. Stanton, Chairman of the Naval Committee of the House of Representatives? State what you know of its circulation.

Ans. He did publish said lecture and at his own expense. I don't know at what cost. There were a great many of them. It was sent to all parts of the Union. There were some thousands distributed. I don't recollect how many.

Testimony read to witness, pronounced correct and witness dismissed; whereupon the Court adjourned until tomorrow morning at 10 o'clock A.M.

Wednesday, December 2 A. D. 1857

Court met pursuant to adjournment. Present: the president, members, Judge Advocate, Mr. Levy and his counsel. The record of yesterday's proceedings was read by the Judge Advocate and approved. And thereupon the said Levy offered in evidence the following Depositions taken upon Interrogatories and cross interrogatories by the Judge Advocate; to the 22nd of which, the said Levy interposed the following objection, to wit:

Mr. Levy, for the reasons states in his objection made on the 17th ult, to the like question as to general reputation, when propounded to Comm. Perry objects to and protests against this cross interrogatory, as illegal and inadmissible.
Signed, U. P. Levy

In the matter of the investigation of the physical, mental, professional and moral fitness of Uriah P. Levy, late a Captain of the Navy of the United States, who was dropped by the operation of the Act of the 28th of February, 1855, and entitled "An Act to Promote the Efficiency of the Navy for the said Naval Service."

PART IV
DEPOSITIONS

Interrogatories

(The answer to each interrogatory to be made on oath, both interrogatories and answers forming part of a deposition proposed to be read in evidence, as per stipulation, before the Naval Court of Inquiry by and before which said investigation is had.)

1st Interrogatory. What is your name, age and occupation?

2nd In what capacity, if at all, are you now, or have you been, connected with the Naval service of the United States? And for how long a time have you been so connected?

3rd Are you acquainted with Uriah P. Levy, above named, and if yea, how long have you been acquainted with him?

4th What has been the degree of such your acquaintance, whether intimate, or how otherwise?

5th What has been the character of such your acquaintance, whether domestic, social, profession, all or any of them? State particularly.

6th Have you personally observed the physical organism, bodily strength, health and capacity of said Uriah P. Levy? If yea, state what has been, as you have observed the same, his physical condition in respect to bodily strength, health and capacity? Has he been, during your acquaintance with him, physically healthful, hardy, active and efficiency, or how otherwise? What in respect to physical health, strength, hardihood, activity and efficiency, is his present state and condition? Supposing him to be now in the sixth-fifth year of his age, how does he compare, in physical vigor, freshness, activity and efficiency, with other persons of like age? Are his present physical capacity and efficiency equal or superior, or interior to those commonly possessed by persons of like age? State fully and particularly in answer to all the matters inquired of by this interrogatory.

7th Have you personally observed the mental and moral traits of character of said Uriah P. Levy? If yea, state as you have observed the same, the character of his mind, as to strength, quickness and activity? Are his mental faculties strong or weak, quick or slow, vigilant or heedless, active or sluggish?

What in respect to strength, quickness, vigilance and activity in his present mental state and condition? Have his mental faculties been at all impaired by age, sickness, intemperance in eating or drinking, or by any other cause, or how otherwise?

State, also, according to your personal knowledge and observation thereof, his moral character and deportment. Is he a man of integrity, fidelity, and truthfulness, or how otherwise? Is he a man of virtuous and temperate life and habits, or how otherwise? Is he a man of courage, moral as well as physical, or how otherwise? Is he a lover of his country, zealous for her honor, interests and rights and prompt to maintain the same, or how otherwise? State fully and particularly, in answer to all the matters inquired of by this interrogatory.

8th Have you personally observed the professional capacity and qualifications for the Naval service of said Uriah P. Levy? If yea, state when and for what periods. In what official grade was he at the time? State also whether you served with him in the Navy of the United States, and if yea, in what capacity and relations, the time when, how long, and how often. In respect to knowledge of and experience in piratical seamanship, and other professional matters, state his attainments and capacity, as you have observed the same. Is he professionally competent to discharge all the duties of the naval service ashore and afloat, or how otherwise? State fully and particularly, in answer to all the matters inquired of by this interrogatory.

9th State whether, in your opinion, founded on your personal knowledge and observation of the character and qualifications of the said Uriah P. Levy, he is physically, mentally, professionally and morally fit for the Naval service of the United States in the grade of Captain in said service, or how otherwise?

Cross Interrogatories
By The Judge Advocate

1. Please to state whether you have ever, and when and where, seen ex-Captain Levy on duty, and on what duty. What is your means of knowledge of the qualities and requirements requisite for the efficient performance of such duty?
2. Do you know the general reputation of the said Levy in respect of the qualities, character, deportment and conduct as an officer and a gentleman? State what that reputation is and what it was prior to his being dropped from the Navy; and whether, in your opinion, a person having such fixed and general reputation is fit to be a Captain of the Navy.

3. Do you know of any fact of "scandalous conduct, tending to the destruction of good morals" or conduct unbecoming an officer and a gentleman by the said ex-Captain Levy? Please to state the same as fully and particularly as if specially interrogated.
4. State any other matter or thing bearing upon this investigation.

J. M. Carlisle, Judge Advocate
Navy Department, August 4, 1857

Thereupon the Court was cleared. The Judge Advocate stated to the Court that he considered the form of Several of the interrogatories *in chief* decidedly objectionable, as well as the *answers* made by some of the witnesses thereto, which are, both in form and substance, altogether argumentative, but under the standing regulation of the Department in relation to the taking of depositions in these investigations, he did not feel authorized to object to them upon these grounds, especially so, as their number is so great, that if objections should be made to every portion thereof which is believed to be objectionable, another week would probably be consumed in disposing of such questions. He further stated that, of strict right, depositions are not admissible in Courts of this description and have in no case been taken and admitted on part of the government. He regarded the objection to the Cross interrogatory as of little practical importance, and the interrogatory objected to as quite as proper as a majority of those in chief.

The Court was of opinion that inasmuch as the admission of depositions in military courts depends entirely upon consent, they must be received as they stand, or rejected altogether.

And thereupon the Court was re-opened and its decision announced by the Judge Advocate.

Mr. Levy, for the reasons heretofore stated by him objects to and protests against the first and second cross interrogatories (below) as illegal and inadmissible.   Signed, U. P. Levy

Cross Interrogatories
By the Judge Advocate

To the witnesses who are, or have been of the Navy:

(1) Has ex-Captain Levy acquired for himself, while in the Naval service, a fixed general reputation in respect of his qualities and deportment as an officer and a gentleman, and do you know what that general reputation is? State what it is, and whether, in your opinion, it materially affects his efficiency in command with officers and men. Explain, if you please, the manner in which such reputation affects his efficiency as a command officer and state whether or not it is calculated to bring discredit upon the Navy.

(2) Do you know what is his general reputation in civil society in respect of moral character and the conduct and bearing of a gentleman? If you do, state what that general reputation is and whether or not it was calculated to bring discredit upon the Navy.

(3) Upon the whole matter stated in your direct and cross interrogatories, is it your opinion, as a Commodore in the U. S. Navy that ex-Captain Levy is a fit and proper person to be restored to the Active List of the Navy? If you think he is, please to give your reasons for that opinion.

(4) State any other matters within your knowledge bearing on this inquiry.
Signed, J. M. Carlisle, Judge Advocate

...
Deposition of Capt. F. H. Gregory, USN

Interrogatories and Cross Interrogatories same as last .

Capt. F. H. Gregory, to the first interrogatory he says:

Ans. My name is Francis Hoyt Gregory. I am nearly 68 years of age. My occupation is that of a Captain in the U. S. Navy.

2nd Ans. I am now in the capacity and holding a commission of a Captain in the U. S. Navy and have been connected with the Naval service of the U. S. as a Mid'n, Acting Master, Lieut., Commander and Captain, since the 16th of January 1809, the date of my first appointment.

3rd Ans. I am acquainted with Uriah P. Levy and have been since some time in the year 1821.

4th Ans. My acquaintance with Uriah P. Levy has always been intimate and friendly whenever circumstances brought us together.

5th Ans. The character of my acquaintance with Uriah P. Levy has been domestic, social and professional. He has always visited my house and family in a social manner. I have not been very intimately acquainted with him professionally, though I have served with him on the same station at New York and in the same Squadron in the West Indies, but not on board the same vessel.

6th Ans. I have had opportunities through a long course of time, of observing the physical organism, bodily strength, health and capacity of said Uriah P. Levy; and have always considered him sound in all of them.. He has been, so far as my observations go, physically healthful, hardy, active and efficient so far as I can judge from frequently seeing him, I consider him now sound in physical, health, strength, hardihood, activity and efficiency. I consider that there are but few men, if any, of my acquaintance, who have arrived at his time of life, that excel him in physical vigor, freshness, activity and efficiency at the present time. I consider his present physical capacity and efficiency superior to those commonly possessed by persons of like age.

7th Ans. I have never observed any defects in the mental and moral traits of character of the said Uriah P. Levy. I have always considered him as possessing strength of quickness of mind and exhibiting great activity and perseverance in every relation of life. I consider his mental faculties as strong, quick, vigilant and active. I consider that, in respect to strength, quickness, vigilance and activity, his present mental state and condition is sound and reliable.

I have no knowledge of any facts or circumstances that would lead to the conviction or belief that his mental faculties have been impaired by age, sickness, intemperance in eating or drinking, or by any other cause. I have always considered him of good moral character and deportment as also a

man of integrity, fidelity and honor. I am not knowing to any acts of doings of his that would lead me to question the virtuous and temperate habits of his life. He is, so far as my knowledge goes, strictly a temperate man. I consider him an undoubted man of courage, moral, as well physical. He has, to my belief, always been a lover of his country, zealous for her honor, interests and rights, and prompt to maintain the same.

8th Ans. I have personally observed the professional qualification for the Naval service of the said Uriah P. Levy; though the opportunities have been few for the length of time I have been acquainted with him. I have seen him on duty in Boston in 1821 or 1822; at several periods in New York though I do not recollect the particular dates, and while he was Executive Officer of the U. S. Brig Spark, employed in the West Indies in 1822 and 1823. When I saw him at those times, he was performing the duties of 1st Lieut. I have not served with him in the Navy of the U. S. otherwise than before related, and never in the same ship. I do not recollect the exact times when, how long, or how often I have seen him engaged in the performance of his professional duties as a Naval officer. From the opportunities I have had of judging of his professional qualifications, attainments and capacity, I have always considered him as having a competent knowledge of and experience in practical seamanship and other professional matters, and I regard him as professionally competent to discharge all the duties of the Naval service, ashore and afloat.

9th Ans. From my personal knowledge and observation of the character and qualifications of the said Uriah P. Levy, it is my opinion that he is physically, mentally, professionally and morally fit for the Naval service of the U. S. in the grade of Captain of said service. Signed,

Answers to Cross Interrogatories

1st Ans. I do not know whether or not ex-Captain Levy has acquired for himself, while in the Naval service, a fixed general reputation in respect of his qualities and deportment as an officer and gentleman. I have always regarded Capt. Levy as a gentleman myself. I do know that there were in years past officers in the Navy entertaining strong prejudices against him, which, I believe, still exist. I know also, that he has friends in the service as well able to judge of his merits who estimate him very differently. So far as my information goes in relation to this matter, the prejudices existing against him originated in his being a Jew. I can not say what his general reputation among the officers is. I have heard but few of them express an opinion on the subject, as many, perhaps, one way as the other. I do not think that he has acquired for himself while in the Naval service, a general reputation that would materially lessen his efficiency in command of officers and men. I, of my own knowledge, know of nothing concerning ex-Captain Levy which is calculated to bring discredit upon the Navy.

2nd Ans. I know of nothing of his general reputation in civil society in respect of moral character, and the tone and bearing of a gentleman, exceptional to either. I believe his reputation in those respects to be good.

3rd Ans. It is my opinion as a Commodore in the U. S. Navy that ex-Captain Levy is a fit and proper person to be restored to the active list of the Navy; for the reasons that I do not know of any act or doing of his which would justly disqualify or exclude him, as, as before stated, I consider him fully qualified and competent for the station.

4th Ans. There are no other matters within my knowledge bearing on this enquiry. Signed, Francis H. Gregory (sworn before Capt. U. S. Navy, C. Robinson, Notary Public)

...

Deposition of Capt. James M. McIntosh, USN, Interrogatories and Cross Interrogatories.

Ans. to 1st Interrogatory. My name is James M. McIntosh. I am 61 years of age. I am a Captain in the United States Navy.

Ans. to 2nd Do. I am connected with the Naval service of the United States as a Captain therein and I have been in the U. S. Navy several years and am at present waiting orders.

Ans. to 3rd Do. I am acquainted with Uriah P. Levy above names and I have been acquainted with him since the year 1822. He was then in command of the U. P. Schooner Revenge, at that time and was the Second Lieut. of the U. S. Brig Enterprise lying in the harbor of Charleston, South Carolina, and while there lost one third from yellow fever, and the attention and kindness of Lieut. Commandant Levy in assisting in nursing and taking care of him was exceedingly gratifying to his mess mates and highly honorable to himself.

Ans. to 4th Do. Previous to Capt. Levy's promotion to a Captain I saw little of him, excepting as I have stated, but since then I have known him more intimately. We met frequently.

Ans. to 5th Do. I have known him professionally as commanding different vessels in the U. States Navy.

Ans. to 6th Do. I have personally observed the physical organism, bodily strength, health and capacity of said Uriah P. Levy. I think that in physical condition in respect to bodily strength, health and capacity. He is equal if not superior to any man of his age I ever knew. During my acquaintance with him he has been physically healthful, hard of active and efficient and he compares most favorably in these expected with persons of a like age. I consider the latter part of the question already answered.

Ans. to 7th Do. I think his mental powers quite equal to those of most others who hold the same rank he did. I do not by any means conceive that his mental faculties are slow or sluggish but the reverse. I cannot say that I have made his mental and moral traits of character a matter of observation but from my acquaintance with him I am enabled to say that I know nothing in these particulars to his disadvantage. His mental faculties have not been at all impaired by age, sickness, and intemperance in eating or drinking or by any other cause. I believe him to be a man of integrity, fidelity and truthfulness, of virtuous and temperate life and habits strictly so. I believe him to be a man of courage, moral as well as physical, a lover of his country, zealous for her honor, interests and sights and prompt to maintain the same.

Ans. to 8th Do. I have observed the professional capacity and qualifications for the Naval service of said Uriah P. Levy. I have known him in command of two vessels, namely, as Lieut. Commanding of the U. S. Schooner Revenge, as previously stated, and as a Commander, in command of the U. S. Sloop of War Vandalia in the West Indies Squadron in 1838 and 39. During the time he commanded the Vandalia she was actively employed cruising in the Gulf of Mexico and West Indies, and so far as I could judge from appearances, the U. S. Schooner Revenge and the U. S. Sloop of War Vandalia were in good order; but the discipline of the Vandalia was complained of by those who were subordinate to Commander Levy. I have never served with ex-Captain Levy, nor under his command. I was a Lieutenant in the Gulf squadron at the time mentioned, part of the time a Lieutenant and part of the time a Commander. I believe him to be practically a seaman and professionally competent to command any ship, so far as my knowledge goes, I believe him professionally competent to discharge all the duties of the Naval service, ashore and afloat.

Ans. to 9th Do. I believe him to be physically, mentally and professionally fit for the Naval service of the United States, in the grade of Captain in said service, as to his moral qualifications I know nothing that would disqualify him.

Answers to Cross Interrogatories by Judge Advocate.

Ans. to 1st Cross Interrogatory. The general reputation of Capt. Levy with a majority of the officers of my acquaintance was unfavorable, but whether that reputation was produced by prejudice or by facts known to them and unknown to me I am unable to say. I do not know that it affected his efficiency in command with officers and men further than the difficulty any officer would find in commanding where such prejudice existed. Whether such reputation would be calculated to bring discredit upon the Navy, would depend upon the manner he executes his command and which would be known to the Department.

Ans to 2nd Do. Since Capt. Levy has resided in New York I have known much of him and his acquaintance and associates have been among gentlemen of the highest standing and so far as I have seen, his tone and bearing has been that of a gentleman and not at all calculated to bring discredit upon the Navy.

Ans to 3rd Do. As a Captain in the U. S. Navy I think he is, and I proud my opinion for answering this question in the affirmative from the fact that when Capt. Levy was nominated by the President of the U. S. Senate for the commission of a Captain, strong opposition was made by those prejudiced against him to his appointment, and after a thorough investigation the Senate of the United States, I have been informed and believe, unanimously confirmed his nomination as Capt. in the U. S. Navy, and I know nothing of any own knowledge or from report which could in any way deteriorate from the judgment of the senate then expressed and also approve any opinion upon my knowledge of him, his course and conduct since he was made a Captain.
Sworn and subscribed before Daniel G. Garrison, Justice of the Peace.

...

And thereupon the said Uriah P. Levy offered in evidence the Deposition of the Hon. George Bancroft, interrogatories and cross interrogatories.

Ans. to 1st Interrogatory. My name is George Bancroft. I am 57 years of age, My occupation is at present of a private character.

Ans. to 2ⁿᵈ Do. I was Secretary of the Navy of the United States from March 1845 to some time in September 1846. I have had no other connection with the United States Navy.

Ans. to 3ʳᵈ Do. I became acquainted with Capt U. P. Levy about 4ᵗʰ March 1845.

Ans. to 4ᵗʰ Do. My acquaintance with Captain Levy was no otherwise intimate than as he constantly importunes me, when Secretary of the Navy, to give him employment suited to his rank, and in particular, when in 1846 the war broke out with Mexico, he was as earnest as an officer could be to get a command during that war.

Ans to 5ᵗʰ Do. My acquaintance with Captain Levy had grown out of any temporary connection with the Navy Department.

Ans to 6ᵗʰ Do. I have always considered the physical capacity and health of Captain Levy to be equal, or superior to those commonly possessed by persons of his age.

Ans to 7ᵗʰ Do. Captain Levy's faculties have seemed to me strong, rather than weak, quick, rather than slow; vigilant, rather than heedless; active, rather than sluggish. I know nothing of their having been impaired, nor do I know anything impeaching his moral character and deportment, his courage or his patriotism; and in answer to the 4ᵗʰ Interrogatory, I have spoken of his desire to be employed in the war against Mexico.

Ans to 8ᵗʰ Do. I never served with Capt. Levy in the Navy of the United States and am unable to speak of his professional attainments and capacity, from personal knowledge.

Ans. to 9ᵗʰ Do. When Secretary of the Navy, I never had cause to doubt, and never doubted Captain Levy's competence to serve the United States, in the grade of Captain. I did not find myself able to give him a command for three reasons. (1) The excessive number of officers of his grade made it impossible to employ all of them who were fit. (2) The good of the service, moreover, seemed to require brining forward officers less advanced in years than most of the Captains; and the law sanctioned that course. (3) **"I perceived a strong prejudice in the service against Captain Levy, which seemed to me, in a considerable part attributable to his being of the Jewish persuasion, and while I, as an Executive Officer had the same liberal views which guided the President and Senate in Commissioning him as a Captain, I always endeavored, in fitting out ships, to have some reference to that harmonious cooperation which is essential to the highest effectiveness."**

Answers to Cross Interrogatories by Judge Advocate

Ans. to 1st Cross Interrogatory. I have never seen ex-Captain Levy on duty. My means of knowledge on the subject of this question were such as were in the reach of a Secretary of the Navy.

Ans to 2nd Do. I know nothing of ex-Captain Levy's general reputation in private life, in respect to the matter, enquires of, until lately, hearing his case discussed, made me enquire as to his general reputation and I round it to be good. I have heard nothing in relation to his general reputation which rendered him unfit to be a Captain in the Navy.

Ans to 3rd Do. I know of no fact to the discredit of ex-Captain Levy.

Ans to 4th Do. I have nothing further to add.
Sworn and subscribed before J. P. Nones, Notary Public

...

And thereupon the said Uriah P. Levy, offered in evidence, the Deposition of Commodore Thomas Ap Catesby Jones, U. P. Levy, Interrogatories and Cross Interrogatories.

Ans. to 1st Interrogatory. Thomas Ap Catesby Jones, age 67, occupation amphibious – sometimes a sailor, sometimes a farmer.

Ans. to 2nd Do. I am now, and have been connected with the Navy, as Midshipman, Lieutenant, Lieutenant Commandant, Master Commandant, Captain and Commander of Squadrons from the 22nd day of November 1805
to the present time, say 52 years lacking one day.

Ans to 3rd Do. I have been acquainted with Captain Uriah P. Levy 41 years.

Ans to 4th Do. Our first acquaintance was through an introduction by a mutual friend on board a Streamer conveying a select party from Baltimore on a visit to the U. S. line of battleship Washington, then at anchor off Annapolis, MD waiting the arrival of Mr. Pinkney, Minister Extraordinary to Naples and Russia. This was in the month of May 1816; from that time to the present moment our relations have been of a friendly character.

Ans to 5th Do. Both social and professional, professionally, on board the frigate United States, in the Mediterranean Station, in the year 1818, when I was First and Levy 3rd or 4th Lieutenant of that ship, then commanded by the last Commodore William M. Crane; socially in Philadelphia, New York, Washington D.C., Richmond, Virginia, and wherever else we chanced to meet. The character of our intercourse had been such whether on or all duty, as well bred gentlemen usually extend to each other, exchanging visits dining together at private and public tables, meeting at evening parties, etc, etc.

Ans to 6th Do. I have never discovered nor suspected any physical, mental, moral or professional deficiency in Capt. Levy. On the contrary, I have always considered him as possessed of an iron frame and unyielding constitution, capable of enduring great labor and exposure equal at least, if not superior, to any other officer of the Navy with whom I am acquainted.

Ans. to 7th Do. Mentally in my judgment Capt. Levy has not many equals left in the grade from which he was ejected. I know of no act of immorality chargeable against Capt. Levy. Capt. Levy is a man of active mind and quick perception, scrupulously jealous of his own, and his Country's rights and honor, neither of which I am sure, can ever be insulted with impunity in his hearing or presence. Whilst Capt. Levy is prompt and always ready to resent insult on all proper occasions, I do not think him reckless or heedless. So far as I have had an opportunity of judging, Capt. Levy is quick, vigilant and prompt in the discharge of all public and private duties; and as to Patriotism and devotion to his country, her institutions and her interests, I know of no one in or out of the Navy, more truly devoted than Captain Levy.

Ans. to 8th Do. Yes. As the 1st Lieut. of a Ship (A. [America]) in a Squadron unequaled before or since for discipline and efficiency, and where the conduct of no officer, or man, could escape observation, Lieut. Levy for several months was 4th and I, 1st Lieut. of the Frigate United States, where he discharges his duty satisfactorily to the Captain as well as to the 1st Lieut., notwithstanding his advent into our ship was attended with such novel and discouraging circumstances, as in justice to Capt. Levy renders it necessary here to record them.

On the arrival of the Franklin of 74 guns and Syracuse in 1818, bearing the broad Pendant of Commodore Charles Stewart, to relieve Commodore Chauncey, then in command of the Mediterranean Squadron, it was understood that Lieut. Levy, a supernumerary on board the Franklin, was to be ordered to the frigate United States, then short of her complement of Lieutenants. Whereupon the wardroom mess without consulting one, determined to remonstrate against Levy's coming aboard, I was called on by a member of the mess to communicate these wishes to Capt. Crane and ask his interference. Astonished at such a proposition, I inquired as to the cause, when I was answered that he was a Jew, and not an agreeable person, and they did not want to be brought in contact with him in our then very pleasant and harmonious mess of some 8 or 9 persons and moreover, that he was an interloper, having entered the Navy as Master to the prejudice of the older midshipmen. Such was the reply, in substance, to any inquiry. I then asked the relater, if her or any member of our mess knew anything of his own knowledge, derogatory in Lieut. Levy as an officer or as a gentleman? The answer was no, but they had heard thus and so, etc, endeavor to point out the difficulties that might result from a procedure so much at variance with military subordination, and the justice due to a brother officer, against whom they had nothing but vague and ill-defined rumors, but my counsel then did not prevail, the remonstrance was made directly to Capt. Crane and by Capt. Crane to Commodore Stewart. Levy soon after reported on board the frigate United States for duty. When Lieut. Levy came on board he asked a private interview with me wishing my advice as to the proper course he ought to pursue under such embarrassing circumstanced. I gave it freely and simply to the effect, viz, do you duty as an officer and a gentleman, be civil to all, however reserved you may choose to be to any, and the first man who observes a different course, answers you, call him to a strict and prompt account. Our messmates were gentlemen and having perceived their error, before Lieut. Levy got on board, had in accordance with my previous advice, determined to receive Lieut. Levy as a gentleman and a brother officer, and to respect and treat him as such, till by his conduct, he should prove himself unworthy. I continued a few months longer on board the frigate United States, as her 1st Lieutenant during the whole of which time Lieut. Levy's conduct and deportment was altogether unexceptionable, and I know that, perhaps with a single exception, those who opposed his joining our mess not only relented, but deeply regretted the false step they has incautiously taken.

The conclusion to which I have arrived through an acquaintance of more than 40 years with Captain Uriah P. Levy, late of the United States Navy, under the varied circumstances, detailed in the foregoing answers, is that Capt. Levy was physically, mentally, morally and professionally competent to fully discharge all the duties, whether ashore or afloat, that could have been reasonably required of a Captain in the Navy, in the year 1855, when he was dropped from the Navy; and if he then was, so far as I can perceive he still is, since his faculties, both physical and mental, appear to remain unimpaired to the present time, and as he is now about 65 years of age, there may be many more years of usefulness yet in store for him.

Answers to Cross Interrogatories by Judge Advocate

Ans. to 1st Cross Interrogatory. Capt. Levy, like all high minded public officers, knowing and faithfully discharging all the duties of their stations, whether in the Navy or Army, or in political stations, who exact like faithfulness from all around and under them, has made enemies. **"To the few clamorous opponents thus made, there may be added, the *Pharisees* of the Navy, who have of late set themselves up guardians of public and Naval morals, and who profess to think that an Israelite is not to be tolerated in or out of the Navy,"** and to those may be further added some who can see nothing praiseworthy or meritorious in certain officers introduced into the Navy as Masters, from the merchant service, subsequent to the reorganization of the Navy in 1800. Captain Levy falling under *these three several unpardonable sins*, it is not surprising that when such influences are active with a few even that a brave and independent man like Capt. Levy who will neither feign, fawn nor flatter, should encounter trials and tribulations in the service. At times there has been much clamor in the Navy against Capt. Levy, which may have been, through its officers, communicated to certain walks in society, but like the case already referred to on board the frigate United States, I believe fair prompt and impartial investigation by disinterested judges have always pronounced in favor of Capt. Levy. In reply to the last member of first cross interrogatory, I have no means of forming an opinion, other than from what I have always understood, that the ship Vandalia, when commanded by Capt. Levy in the West Indies or Gulf Squadron, was considered the man of war of the Squadron, although Capt. Levy has among his officers, the most satisfactory in the Navy at that day. The selection of Levy's ship, by Commodore Dallas, as the bearer of his board pendant, may be received as a fair interpretation of this Commodore's opinion of Capt. Levy and his efficiency as a Commander.

Ans. to 2nd Do. Answered by my answers to direct interrogatories in this case and by the foregoing answer to 1st cross interrogatory.

Ans to 3rd Do. Upon the whole matter stated in my direct and cross interrogatories, *it is my opinion*, as a Commodore in the U. S. Navy, that ex-Captain Levy *is a fit and proper person to be restored to the active list of the Navy*. My opinion is strengthened and amply sustained by the Committee on Naval Affairs in the U. S. Senate, in the year when Commander Levy's nomination for promotion to Captain in the Navy, was warmly opposed by the clique which still oppose him. On that occasion it is understood that all complaints and allegations on record at the Navy Department were before the Committee of the Senate which after thorough examination of the charged against Commander Levy, recommended its confirmation, and he was accordingly confirmed by the Senate and Commissioned by the President of the United States, as a Captain in the Navy, from which time to the 13th day of September 1855, he held his said commission without having been called into active service, and consequently without having done anything. So far as my knowledge extends, to forfeit a just title to his commission of Captain thus and so confirmed by the President and Senate of the United States, and further this deponent sayeth not.
Sworn and subscribed before, W. W. Ball, Judge Advocate

Finding and Report
And thereupon the Court, upon consideration, does find that the said Levy is morally, mentally, physically and professionally fit for the Naval service, and does respectfully report that he ought to be restored to the active list of said Navy. In testimony whereon we have hereunto set our hands, this 24th day of December, A. D., 1857.   L. Kearney, President
G. W. Stover, Member
J. F. Montgomery, Capt. Member

Attest: R. R. Little, Judge Advocate

PART V
MR. PRESIDENT AND GENTLEMEN OF THE COURT

My defence so far as it depends on the examinations of the evidence you have received, is before you. I have shown what I promised in my opening remarks. First, my nautical experience and education, as a seaman, prior to my entering the Navy; secondly, the history and character of my connection with the Naval service; thirdly, the gross injustice of the exparte sentence by means of which I was dismissed from that service; fourthly, the provisions made by Congress in the act under which this Court is organized, for the reviewing of that sentence; and lastly that it is the solemn duty of this Court under the law by which it is governed and upon the evidence before it, to report to the President, as the result of this investigation, any physical, mental, professional and moral fitness for the Naval service and that I ought to be restored to the active list of the grade from which I was dropped.

Here, perhaps, I ought to stop. But the peculiarities of my case – the importance and far-reaching interest of the principles it involves, require what I hope you will allow one, a few additional remarks.

That the case alleged against one by the government was wholly unsupported by any significant evidence; that the little it contained to my prejudice has been perfectly repelled by me; and that I have made out a complete defense against the attempt to justify my dismissal, and an affirmative title to my restoration by the people on my past. These I regard as undeniable propositions.

And yet there are those connected with the Navy, who notwithstanding the proofs I have produced, are still hostile to my restoration. This, it would be in vain to deny to others, or to attempt to conceal from myself. If any of these should dare to obtrude upon you the opinion or the wish that I should not be restored, in being restored should not be placed upon the active list, you have but to refer him to the oath that you have taken, to silence and rebuke him. Permit me – not that I suppose that you can have forgotten its terms but because of their peculiar pertinency to my case – to quote all the words of this oath. It not only requires you as before remarked well and truly to examine and inquire, according to the evidence, into the matter now before you, but to do this "*without partiality or prejudice.*" This oath though exceedingly brief, is exceedingly comprehensive and precise. The law-makers who framed it well knew the special dangers to which Courts of Inquiry are exposed. Partiality towards influential prosecutors and accusers – prejudices against the accused – against these, the oath solemnly warns you; and if ever there was a case in which such an admonition was right and reasonable, this is that case. The Government with its vast power and influence is, in name, at least, my prosecutor.

Men in high places, who have once done my grievous wrong, are interested to present the remedying of that wrong. There are others not without their influence, who by their activity in support of the wrong, and in opposition to the remedy, have a common interest with my prosecutors – whoever these may be.

Never, on the other hand, was there a man, in the ranks of our profession, against whom, in the breasts of certain members of that profession, prejudices so unjust and yet so strong, have so long and so incessantly rankled. Such, too, are the origin and character of these prejudices as to make them, of all others, the most inveterate and unyielding. The prejudice felt by men of little minds, who think themselves by the accidental circumstances of wealth or ancestry, better than the less favored of their fellows; the prejudice of caste which looks down on the man who, by honest toil, is the maker of his own fortunes; this prejudice is stubborn as well as bitter, and of this I have had, as you have seen by the proofs, my full share. But this is placable and transient compared with that generated and nourished by religious intolerance and bigotry.

The first article of the amendments to the Constitution of the United States explicitly declares that "Congress shall make no law respecting an establishment of religion or prohibiting the free exercise thereof; showing by its place no less than by its heritage how highly freedom of conscience was valued by the founders of our republic.

In the constitutions of the several states now in force, the like provision is contained. In this respect, we have been honored by the friends of liberty and of human rights, as in the sole exception in Christendom. An eminent British writer about forty years ago in the ablest of their reviews used in reference to this point the following language. "They have fairly and completely, and probably forever, extinguished that spirit of religious persecution which has been the employment and the curse of mankind for four or five centuries, not only that persecution which imprisons and scourges for religious oppression, but the tyranny of incapacitation, which by disqualifying from civil offices, and cutting a man off from the lawful objects of ambition, endeavors to strangle religious freedom in silence and to enjoy all the advantages, without the blood, and noise and fire of persecution.

In this particular, the Americans are at the head of all the nations of the world.

Little did the author of this generous tribute to our country dream, that within a period so short, it should come to be a question in America, whether a Jew should be tolerated in the Navy! Still less could he have dreamt that at the very moment when in Great Britain, according to advices just received, a representative of the illustrious House of Russell imminent by his services in the cause of freedom, of education, and of justice, is giving himself with the full assent of his government to the work of Jewish emancipation, the spectacle should be presented, in this land of equal rights and equal laws, of an officer whose services, Israelite though he was, were gladly accepted by his government in the hour of national peril; of an officer long tried in his country's service, who had given to that service the freshness of his youth and the vigor of his manhood – one proved by half a century of witnesses, still preeminently quality therefore by his patriotism, his valor, his fidelity, and his ability of such an officer struggling to regain the privilege wrongfully arrested from him, of serving his country while he lives and of dying on her defence, that to his success in this struggle there should be one and but one serious impediment; and this should be found in the fact of his religion. And yet this is the case before you. My case is the case of every Israelite in the Union—I need not speak to you of their number. But I may speak of the fact, that they are unsurpassed by any other portion of our people, in loyalty to the Constitution and to the Union; by their quiet support of our laws and constitutions; by the cheerfulness with which they contribute their share of the brethrens, and by the liberal donations many of them have made to promote the general interests of education and of charity; and in some instances along with these, of which the name of Judah's honor will remind you of charities controlled by Christians, and sometimes exclusively devoted to the benefit of Christians. Again, how rarely does one of my brethren—either of foreign birth or American descent—become a charge on your state or municipal treasuries? How largely do they all contribute to the activities of trade, to the interest of commerce, to the stock of public wealth?

Are all these to be placed under the ban of incapacitation? And is this to be done while we retain in our Constitution the language I have quoted? Is that language to be spoken to the ear, but broken to the hope of any race? Are the thousands of Israel and the ten thousands of Judah in their dispersion throughout the earth who look to America as a land bright with promise; are they now to learn, to their sorrow and disarray, that we too, have sunk into the mire of religious intolerance and bigotry? And are American Christians now to begin the persecution of the Jew. Of the few who stands among them the representatives of the patriarchs and prophets to whom were committed the oracles of God, the Jew from whom they received these articles and who is the living witness of their truth, the Jew of whom came the founders of their religion, the Jew to whom Christians themselves believe, these yet pertain "exceeding great and precious promises in whose fulfillment are bound up the hopes, not merely of the remnant of Israel but of all the races of men?

And think not if you once enter on this career, that is can be limited to the Jew that is my case today if you yield to this injustice, may tomorrow be that of the Roman Catholic, or the Unitarian, the Presbyterian, or the Methodist, the Episcopalian or the Baptist. There is inborne safeguard, that

as to be found in an honest, wholehearted, inflexible support of the service, the just, the impartial guarantee of the Constitution. I have the fullest confidence that you will faithfully adhere to this guarantee and therefore with like confidence I leave my destiny in your hands.

                                                                Signed, U. P. Levy

Index to Supplemental Information

I. Records of the Royal Navy –
  Admiralty Historical Section; War of 1812
  Log Book – HMS Leonidas – August 12, 1813
  Prisoner of War Record – Uriah Phillips Levy

II. Excerpt from Last Will of Uriah Phillips Levy
  Re: Estate at Monticello, Virginia

III. Events [dates] Extracts from Naval Service

  Record after Court of Inquiry of 1857

IV. Epilogue

V. About the Author – Melvin A. Young

I.
Extracts from Log Book HMS Leonidas, 13 Aug. 1813
...
Bearings and Distances at noon... Cape Cornwall S. 238, 11 Leagues
...
...Fired a shot to bring her too. 9:15 hove too and spoke to her, hailed to be from Liverpool to London but on boarding her proved to be the Ship Betsy from the West Indies, a Prize to the United States Brig Argus taken off Landry Isle yesterday, found the Prize Master [Levy] had scuttled her, lowered the boats and sent the carpenters on board and stopped the leak...
...
Took the prisoners out ...

Extract of Prisoner of War Record
...

13 August 1813 – Confined from the United States Ship of War Argus...taken rom Prize belonging to the Argus by the Leonidas...Uriah P. Levy, Sailing Master...

II.

Excerpt from His Last Will and Testament

...

I give, devise and bequeath my Farm and Estate at Monticello in Virginia, formerly belonging to President Thomas Jefferson together with all the rest and residue of my estate, real personal or mixed not hereby disposed of wherever or however situated to the People of the United States or such persons as Congress shall appoint to receive it.

...

[ED] At the time of his death in March 1862, Captain Uriah Phillips Levy was on active duty with the United States Navy. Virginia had seceded from the Union and was part of the Confederacy. The legal issues on this fact and subsequent surviving family issues took years to resolve. Jefferson Monroe Levy, inspired by his uncle's actions, began to restore the place to its former beauty. In 1923 the Thomas Jefferson Memorial Foundation was formed and it acquired Monticello from Jefferson Monroe Levy.

...

III.
EVENTS [DATES]
EXTRACTS FROM SERVICE RECORD
DEPARTMENT OF NAVY

After Court of Inquiry 1857

1858 – January 29 – Restored to Active List as Captain from March 29, 1844

...

1860 – January 7 – Ordered to Command Of Mediterranean Squadron with Title of Flag Officer; to hoist flag on "Macedonia"

...

1860 – February 21 – HOISTED FLAG ON USS MACEDONIA

...

HENCEFORTH: COMMODORE URIAH PHILLIPS LEVY, CAPTAIN USN

...

[Ed Note] Captain Uriah Phillips Levy served in the United States Navy in the American Civil War until his death on March 22, 1862.

...

IV.

EPILOGUE

Uriah Phillips Levy left a legacy of a United States Naval tradition that transcended the 19th century and well into the 20th century from generation to generation.

Extended related family members of Uriah P. Levy: Those who have attended the United States Naval Academy

Class	Name	Service
1864	Raphael J. Moses	Res 1861, Officer in CSN
1881	Franklin J. Moses	Col. USMC – Died AD 1914
1890	Lawrence H. Moses	Col. USMC – (Ret.)
1892	Stanford E. Moses	Capt. USN- (Ret.)
1902	William L. Moses	Lt. Cmdr. USN – (Ret.)
1906	Edward S. Moses	Lt. Cmdr. USN – (Ret.)
1920	William M. Moses	Capt. USN – (Ret.)
1923	Lionel B. Moses	Hon. Disc. – Phy. Dis.
1930	Walter C. Moses	Sep. (Acad. – def.) Ret. Comdr. - USNR
1931	McDonald Moses	Lt. (jg) – USN - (Ret.)

Additional members of these families served as United States Naval Officers in war and peace in the 19th and 20th centuries.

In particular, Raphael J. Moses, Esq. (of Boulder, Colorado, age 95 - 2008), who as an officer on board the USS Bush, (DD529), on April 5, 1945, which was sunk during the Battle of Okinawa when the ship was struck by three Japanese Kamikaze's. Lt. Raphael J. Moses was rescued after nine (9) hours in the water.

...

On September 18, 2005, at the United States Naval Academy, Annapolis, Maryland, THE COMMODORE URIAH P. LEVY CENTER AND JEWISH CHAPEL was dedicated.

...

L'Dor V'Dor   q.e.d.

ABOUT THE EDITOR
MELVIN A. YOUNG

Mel Young is a longtime resident of Chattanooga, Tennessee, site of the Battles of Chickamauga, Lookout Mountain and Missionary Ridge. He is a 1952 graduate of the United States Military Academy and served as an infantry officer during the Korean conflict. He has served on the boards of numerous professional, civic and cultural boards in the Chattanooga community and the State of Tennessee.

A West Point graduate, Mel Young has spent nearly 25 years researching old books, newspapers and historical records seeking the names of Jewish soldiers in the War Between the States for his first book, *Where They Lie*. That book (UPA-1991) documents the stories of more than 600 Jewish soldiers of the Civil War... where they fought, how they were honored and where they lie buried.

His second book, *Last Order of the Lost Cause*, (UPA-1996) is the story of the southern Jewish family of Raphael Jacob Moses, Major, CSA and his family, before, during and after the Civil War; and the unfinished mystery of the "Confederate Gold."

The third book, *Bitter Tears I Shed for Thee*, (Hamilton Books – 2006) is a collection of fifteen short but very true stories, of heroes (and a heroine) during the Civil War and into the Indian Wars. These people pioneered the way for assimilation of American Jewry into the mainstream of American way of life.

This fourth book, *Uriah*, also sets an example of the difficulty faced in being accepted as true Americans and of a minority religion.

www.ingramcontent.com/pod-product-compliance
Lightning Source LLC
Chambersburg PA
CBHW021411290426
44108CB00010B/477